Science Policies in International Perspective – the experience of India and The Netherlands

Science Policies in International Perspective
– the experience of India and The Netherlands

Papers from the Indo–Dutch Workshop on Science Policy, New Delhi, 5–6 September, 1988

Editors
P.J. Lavakare and J. George Waardenburg
Associate Editor
W. Hutter

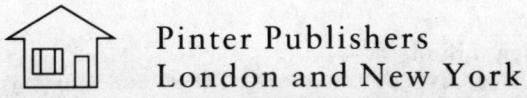
Pinter Publishers
London and New York

Dedicated to Jawaharlal Nehru,
who introduced Science Policy as a Scientific Policy

© Pinter Publishers 1989

First published in Great Britain in 1989 by
Pinter Publishers Limited
25 Floral Street, London WC2E 9DS

British Library Cataloguing in Publication Data

A CIP catalogue record for this book is available from the
British Library
ISBN 0–86187–826–4

Library of Congress Cataloging-in-Publication Data

Indo-Netherlands Workshop on Science Policy (1988: New Delhi, India)
    Science policies: an international perspective: papers from the
Indo-Netherlands workshop on Science Policy, New Delhi, September
5–6, 1988 / edited by P.J. Lavakare and J. George Waardenburg :
associate editor, W. Hutter.
    p. cm.
    ISBN 0–86187–826–4
    1. Science and state — India — Congresses. 2. Technology and state —
India — Congresses. 3. Science and state — Netherlands — Congresses.
4. Technology and state — Netherlands — Congresses. I. Lavakare, P.
J. II. Waardenburg, J. George. III. Hutter, W. IV. Title.
Q127.I4152   1988
338.95406 — dc20   89-27974
                                                                CIP

Filmset by Mayhew Typesetting, Bristol
Printed and bound in Great Britain by Biddles Ltd of Guildford and Kings Lynn.

Contents

List of contributors

Rais Ahmed: Former Vice-Chairman, University Grants Commission, New Delhi

Stuart Blume: Professor of Science Dynamics, University of Amsterdam

C.M. Cooper: Professor of Development Studies, Institute of Social Studies, The Hague

Sukh Dev: Director, Malti-Chem Research Centre, Nandesari, Baroda

Vasant Gowariker: Secretary, Department of Science and Technology, Government of India, New Delhi

W. Hutter: Secretary, Advisory Council for Science Policy, Raad van Advies voor het Wetenschapsbeleid (RAWB), The Hague

Ashok Jain: Director, National Institute of Science, Technology and Development Studies, Council of Scientific and Industrial Research, New Delhi

P.J. Lavakare: Adviser, Department of Science and Technology, Government of India, New Delhi

H.J. van der Molen: Director General, Netherlands Organization for Scientific Research, Nederlandse Organisatie voor Wetenschappelijk Onderzoek (NWO), The Hague

F. Prakke: Policy Analyst, Centre for Technology and Policy Studies, Apeldoorn; Professor of Economics and Technical Change, University of Limburg, Maastricht

S.K. Shrivastava: Joint Educational Adviser, Department of Education, Government of India, New Delhi

E. van Spiegel: Director General for Science Policy, Ministry of Education and Science, Zoetermeer

K.V. Swaminathan: Adviser, Department of Scientific and Industrial Research, Government of India, New Delhi

S.R. Valluri: Former Director, National Aeronautical Laboratory, Council of Scientific and Industrial Research, Bangalore

J. George Waardenburg: Professor of Development Planning, Centre for Development Planning, Erasmus University, Rotterdam

A.D. Wolff-Albers: Member, Scientific Council for government Policy Wetenschappelijke Raad voor het Regeringsbeleid (WRR), The Hague

Foreword

The Netherlands and India have fairly different cultural and economic backgrounds: the former is a small developed country with Western traditions and the latter a large developing country with its own traditional Eastern culture. In spite of this divergence we have found, in the field of science and technology, that we can learn a lot from each other for mutual benefit and, we hope, for the larger good of the international community. Such mutual benefit can only come by striving together towards this objective. A joint workshop on a subject like science policy is a step in the process of bringing our two countries together to enhance mutual understanding and cooperation.

The international aspects of science and technology have to be kept in view while dealing with national polices in pursuit of modern science and technology, which continue to advance at a rapid pace. National goals, no doubt, will be a major guiding force in our perception of policy issues. Having agreed to employ the tools of science and technology for the overall benefit of our societies, it is most interesting to explore together the myriad facets of science policy.

Our respective policies have so far played a dual role: we have striven to foster and promote research activities in science and technology in areas of interest and concern to our scientists, at the same time we have worked hard to ensure that science and technology are harnessed to programmes which are geared to fulfilling the needs of our societies. Our governments have assumed a major responsibility in supporting these initiatives and aspirations. In this process our educational and research institutions, as well as our industries, can play appropriate roles. In trying to achieve these dual objectives we must also strive to provide an environment of peace and understanding which will enhance the prosperity of our two countries.

The India–Netherlands Joint Committee on Science and Technology recognized this central role which our science policies have to play when outlining the collaborative programmes between our two countries. Such programmes in the fields of instrumentation, biotechnology, remote sensing and astronomy have already been identified and our scientists have already initiated activities in most of these areas. We believe that the science policy workshop held in New Delhi on 5–6 September 1988 will further stimulate the interest of scientists in these areas.

We are happy to see that the various issues raised during this workshop are being disseminated through the publication of this book, potentially forming the basis for many more mutually beneficial ventures in the future.

E. van Spiegel and Vasant Gowariker, Co–Chairmen,
Indo-Netherlands Joint Committee on Science and Technology

Introduction: the challenge of science policy

Science policy is one of the most challenging aspects of government policy. There is no dearth of arguments that science has a great impact on societies, that it is the basis of much material progress but also deeply influences the people's mental fabric, changing their views on life and on the world and that it can be a great force for development. But the blessings of science are not undisputed. The same area of research which has released seemingly unlimited sources of energy has also unleashed forces of unimaginable destruction. The application of apparently beneficial inventions and production processes, based on scientific research, recently has also given rise to environmental degradation which threatens to destroy the basic conditions for human life and has already accelerated a global growth process giving rise to appalling disparities in welfare levels between and within countries.

The basic ambiguity in the impact of science on society should in our opinion, however, not deter us from seeking to employ the positive opportunities of science and technology. It rather strengthens the challenging character of this search and the need to do it with a warm heart but a cool mind, that is enthusiastically but not uncritically. The difficulties and opportunities for this search have been well documented by J. Irvine and B.R. Martin (1984), while M. Gibbons and P. Gummet (eds) (1984) also provide useful material.

This first conclusion on the positive potential of science confronts us only with the next challenge, to transform this positive appreciation of science into a vision on science policy which is in harmony with the needs and aspirations of our societies and with the national goals reflecting these needs and aspirations. The benefits of science and technology for a nation can only be reaped at the cost of considerable efforts and resources. This charges the science policy makers, both those within the government and those who lend direction to the development of science and technology outside the government, with a high responsibility to develop a philosophy of science and science policy that is responsive to its great potential both as intellectual endeavour and as servant of mankind; and yet is not carried away by its dazzling prospects to the point of unlimited support for scientific research beyond the true long-term interests of society in pure, strategic and applied research (S. Blume, J. Bunders, *et alia* (eds), 1987). The concept of strategic research used here is that which falls between pure and applied research: it is 'basic' research carried out with the expectation that it will produce a broad base of knowledge likely to form the background to the solution of recognized current or future practical problems.

It is precisely because of the impact of science and technology that science policy has increasingly moved to the centre of government policies in the developed as well as the developing countries. Developments in science and technology are taking place rapidly, the role played by science as well as technology is increasingly being debated. While science continues to keep its international character and its appeal to the intellectual community, technology, which is based on it, is affecting the daily lifestyles of people, but in different measures with respect to developed and developing societies. In terms of changes in these societies implications of science and technology are raising some very fundamental issues about the direction and the desirability of the extent of these changes and about our capability to control them in a manner consistent with national values as expressed by our development goals or otherwise. It is aptly stated that while 'science explores, technology executes'. The question of whether we are getting ourselves into a 'technology fix' is sufficiently unsettling to make us stop and ask ourselves just what are the objectives of these exciting adventures in science and technology. The decisions about the extent of support to be provided for the growth of these activities is to a large extent, being taken by governments, and the policies to be followed in this regard are being reviewed from time to time. The global and all-embracing nature of science and technology has meant that such policies for the pursuit of science and technology (referred to in short as 'science policies') cannot be restricted merely to looking at investment decisions within the national economic framework, but have to take into account the impact on the social milieu of a particular society and the overall international socio-economic environment. It is against the background of such considerations as indicated in this section that national policies towards a R & D system have to be developed, a concern of planners and decisionmakers in developed as well as developing countries. For this aspect the papers in M. Gibbons *et alia* (1984) are quite useful reading.

This leads on to the question of whether the process of science policymaking can learn anything from the relatively well-established methodology of economic development planning and of economic policy preparation. We shall dwell for a while on this question here, coming largely to a negative conclusion, but later on we will argue that in connecting science policy with industrial policy the relationship between science and economics as such is more evident, leading to simple formulas for science policy.

Why is science policymaking very different in nature from the making of an economic (development) policy? First of all, an economic development policy deals after all with more or less directly tangible objects, whatever difficulties economists and statisticians may have with recording and evaluating all items (including the notoriously elusive service-sector) which contributes to human welfare.

A small part of these tangible items has a 'public good' character. A pure 'public good' item is defined here as an item which is not used exclusively by one person or institution, such as a radio or TV broadcast, parks, lighthouses, national defence, etc. (J. George Waardenburg, 1989). The valuation of 'public good' items at market prices presents a well-known difficulty, the reason for valuating these (mostly public) services in the statistics at their cost price. Also demand for these items does not easily reveal itself in the market by a willingness to pay for them. Therefore, their provision in economic policy is largely based on 'informed judgement' or political decisions.

The direct outcome of science policy, even in the most concrete form of actual research results, is essentially not directly tangible and has moreover this very character of public good. Valuation of research results at their cost price, i.e. at their cost price of personnel and equipment involved in their research, denies the very essence of the value of research results, both with respect to enlightening the public and in terms of providing the basis for making material artifacts and solving concrete problems thereby. Moreover, the need for the greater part of research results (the basic or fundamental strategical part) cannot be revealed by any private willingness to pay for it. On the other hand, there exists for another aspect of research results — the applied and development part — the possibility of an indirect valuation of some research results via the material and marketable products resulting from their application. A lot of devising or 'informed judgement' in science policy uses implicitly, or explicitly, such a train of thought. This, however, does not take away the essentially intangible and public-good character of research results or of science in general which makes science policy somewhat different in nature from economic policy.

Another difference between economic policy and science policy might rest with the system *vis-à-vis* which these policies are operating. An economy, notwithstanding all its especially dynamic complexities and its intricate boundaries and overlaps with socio-political and cultural dimensions of society, constitutes a system that is relatively known and which reacts relatively predictably to policy measures, in particular in the form of material (dis)incentives and opportunities or restrictions. A country's R & D system, in contrast to an economy, consists of researchers, institutes, networks, values and incentive systems, patterns of behaviour and planning whose interaction is much less known, less researched and possibly also much less regularly predictable than an economy. This makes all those who wield policy instruments used to influence or steer such a system a little more dubious about their actual impact. We have no difficulty recognizing the validity of doubts cast by researchers in the sociology of science about the ability to influence the R & D system by external measures, given its strong internal motivations and dynamics.

This somewhat impermeable character of the R & D system is strengthened by the difficulty to perceive it, or parts of its activities or its results, without employing the very experts and expertise which are so much part and parcel of the system itself. Again, here is a considerable, third, difference from the economic system where results and several other elements can be easily observed by all people who can look and count, and especially count money.

The methodology of economic development planning and of economic policy (Tinbergen, 1952; Chakravarty, 1958) rests largely on the ability to translate general aims of policy into reasonably concrete aggregate targets of policy (as for example in terms of growth of national income:

employment, poverty elimination, price stability or balance of payments); to derive from these aggregate targets more disaggregated ones (such as concrete projects); to design and handle (packages of) policy instruments (for example expenditures, tariffs, licences, training, legal, or information activities) on the basis of knowledge of the economic system and of its reactions to policy measures in order to steer the system into the direction of the disaggregated targets. This formulation holds true even if the system is very dispersed and largely stochastic, and if the measures are only conceived of as incremental and adaptive, while economists also make useful distinctions between short-term (one to three years), medium-term (three to five years) and long-term (over five years) policies, according to the length of the period within which the instruments handled have their impact on the system. Science policy methodology could certainly profit from the logic of economic development policy preparation in clearly distinguishing aims and instruments of policy; the science and technology (S & T) system and the policy which tries to influence it; and short-, medium- and long-term policies.

But the S & T system has at least three difficulties in following economic policy methodology as indicated above: (a) it cannot translate general aims so concretely into targets because of the intangibility and public-good character of its results, (b) the S & T system is less known and stable in its performance and reaction to policy measures and (c) the observation of the S & T system and of its results requires a strong expertise from within that system itself. For example purely scientific quality of research proposals or results cannot be judged by consumers in a market, but only by experts within the system. Also in order to evaluate the societal value of research areas, programmes and projects, broad consultations have to be held. In The Netherlands, for example, ten years of useful experience has been gained from semi-permanent sector councils composed of representatives from the research world, the government and consumers which advise the government and researchers on useful directions in certain sectors like agriculture, development (cooperation), research environment and health care from a societal point of view (Snellen, 1983). All in all, both the evaluation of scientific quality and that of societal usefulness of research results require much more than market signals which place constraints on the possibility of commercialization of S & T. Therefore the subject of science policy presents a considerable intellectual challenge because of its relative complexity and intangibility. The contributions to this book reflect these characteristics.

Notwithstanding the debates on the different methodologies and premises of a science policy and an economic policy, it is evident that the economic and industrial development of a particular country is increasingly dependent on the changes taking place in the global science and technology scene. While the objectives and policies for industrial development could be expressed in terms of an equitable provision of goods and services, the objectives of a science policy cannot be considered as directly synonymous to or congruent with those of industrial development, even though at first sight they may appear to be closely coupled. Technological developments in one part of the world, achieved as a result of specific policy imperatives in that part of the world may have undesired impacts on the development of another part of the world. Industrial growth achieved through use of newer technologies in one country may result in stunting the natural growth of industrial activity in another country whose markets may suddenly be affected due to introduction of new technologies from outside. The rapid pace of industrial growth in one country may bring about an economic (and perhaps political) dependence of other countries on it and may thus have an undesirable impact on their sovereignty. The science and technology policies have clearly to be examined in an international perspective rather than being treated as isolated, national policies.

The process of bringing about development or growth through the pursuit of a national science policy is also critically dependent on the strategy adopted for long-term and sustaining growth and cannot be a one-time measure, involving *ad hoc* introduction of technological inputs from outside. If the policy does not provide for suitable mechanisms for absorption and adoption of such an external input, its introduction may set in train a process of artificial and short-term growth which, while providing apparently quick returns, may, in the long term, result in a permanent dependency syndrome, eroding an indigenous decisionmaking capacity which is vital to a self-reliant development process. The industrial development policy must therefore have strong linkages with the science policy, which should include in its ambit the objective of building up the necessary manpower to ensure the assimilation of technological inputs used for industrial growth. Science policy must therefore include a strong element of human resource development. With growing international competition among the industrial giants, the developing nations will find themselves at the mercy of these enterprises if their own negotiating capacity through indigenous R & D efforts is not ensured.

Conversely, the effectiveness of indigenous R & D efforts can be enlarged considerably if the practical use of its results can be enhanced, wherever appropriate. Experience shows that such a practical use is by no means ensured simply by producing suitable research results for it. Even after that several mechanisms stand in the way which require well-designed policies and channels to overcome them. If the research is motivated by practical considerations, such obstacles may be less severe.

Then in the design of an actual science policy there is the underlying question: for whom? Is it a policy which defines which areas of science should be pursued by the scientific community (i.e. policy for science) or is it a policy which examines the broad role of science (and technology) in accruing benefits to the society — not just material benefits but benefits which may be measured in terms of progress towards a cultured, just and humane society. Remarkably both India and The Netherlands, who agreed to hold a joint workshop on the topic of science policy have to a certain extent recognized these challenges in science policy formulation and already taken steps to enumerate these policy directives in their respective national policy documents.

Pandit Jawaharlal Nehru, India's first prime minister, articulated these objectives in what he called the Scientific Policy Resolution, which was approved by India in 1958. The policy rightly stresses the dual responsibility of fostering and promoting scientific activity in all its aspects, basic as well as applied, creating an environment conducive to these pursuits and at the same time stresses the objective of accruing benefits to the society through the application of scientific knowledge. It is perhaps more concerned with people than with science *per se*. Recently in India an approach to a plan for the year 2000 was being formulated in which the role of science and technology was being identified.

In The Netherlands, after the first Science Policy Document had been accepted by Parliament in the mid-seventies, the major changes in the environment of the R & D system in general which are forthcoming and the imminent removal of frontiers within the European community in particular were the reasons for initiating a national debate on a new document, 'Towards a science policy for the nineties', which was published in its preliminary version in the summer of 1988.

Such discussions on science policy in both countries took place against a background of a much longer involvement in economic planning which provided a certain common experience for both countries notwithstanding their considerable differences in several respects. The Netherlands was one of the first Western countries to set up, immediately after World War II, a central planning bureau. Its work has been directed at stabilizing policies in the re-emerging and growing economy rather than at development planning itself. Prof. J. Tinbergen provided the initiative and first leadership for this bureau which was conceived in his pioneering work on development dynamics and comprehensive macro-economic modelling of an economy for which he was later awarded the first Nobel prize in economics. India has been widely recognized for its early, original and thorough planning framework and organization under the initial inspiration and leadership of Dr P.C. Mahalanobis. This structure has continued to provide the basis for India's development policy (Chakravarty, 1987).

These developments in the two countries provided the background for the Indo-Dutch workshop on Science Policy in September 1988 in New Delhi, under the auspices of the Indo-Dutch Joint Committee on Science and Technology, set up by the two governments to promote bilateral cooperation in the various fields of science and technology. As co-chairmen of the workshop and now as editors of this joint publication, we have had a unique opportunity of bringing together — from both sides — a group of scientists, engineers, economists, managers and decisionmakers to prepare background papers on various facets of science policy issues which concerned them all and which in turn were affecting the development of the two countries. The complexity of the subject of science policy had to be simplified for the limited duration of the workshop and with some hesitation we confined our deliberations to the following areas:

(a) Science policy and national goals
(b) National policies towards R & D systems
(c) Practical use of the results of R & D systems
(d) International Dimension of R & D and International Cooperation

We are aware of the considerable overlap which exists as we move from one topic to another but none the less we hope that the individual papers provide an opportunity to understand the complexities of the issues involved within the framework of international cooperation between two countries which appear to have widely differing socio-economic backgrounds. The papers and the discussions which follow have clearly brought out some common issues of concern which reflect, in our view, the international character of science and technology. If international cooperation in science and technology is one of the major objectives to be pursued by the developing and the developed countries, we believe that mutual understanding of such complex issues is vital, and we hope that this book will to some extent help towards that goal.

Each of the topics listed above has been looked at by individuals who have been associated with their respective national activities for a long time. Surprisingly enough the issues which surfaced had considerable commonality and we have briefly highlighted these in the beginning of each Part. As editors, we have, however, not attempted — and indeed it would be beyond our competence to do so — to provide solutions to the various issues and questions raised, but we are certain that raising them has helped in stimulating the discussions at the workshop. The discussions 'cleared the air', to provide an understanding of viewpoints and very often resulted in identifying common approaches which are being followed independently by the two countries. We therefore not only asked the authors of the papers to revise them in the light of the discussion, but also decided to include the highlights of these discussions in this publication, and in some cases we even invited special contributions in the form of brief papers based on oral interventions during the workshop which we feel have enriched the debate on these topics. To the authors of the papers, discussion summaries and additional contributors we express our gratitude, with a special word of thanks to Dr W. Hutter, general secretary of the Advisory Council for Science Policy (RAWB) in The Netherlands, who ably helped us in the preparation of this book as co-editor.

The different socio-economic backgrounds of the two countries must be taken into account when we try to understand the science policies being pursued by them. The existing and the proposed policy instruments in each country had to be studied while commenting on each other's science policies. Accordingly, we have included in the book 'country reports', fairly detailed accounts of science and technology policies in the two countries. We hope that publication will therefore provide potential collaborators in the two countries — and indeed members of the international community who might like to study these two countries — an opportunity for better understanding the science and technology potential and aspirations of The Netherlands and India.

This publication would not have materialized had it not been for the initiative and encouragement provided on both sides by those who were responsible for the implementation of the Indo-Dutch cooperation programme in science and technology. The commitment of the two sides was aptly demonstrated by the statements made by the two co-chairmen of the joint committee and for the sake of completeness of this unique exercise we have reproduced these statements in this publication (see appendices).

In conclusion, we would like humbly to dedicate this work to the memory of an outstanding world leader, Jawaharlal Nehru, India's first prime minister, whose birth centenary falls in 1989, and who was an architect of the basic concepts of science policy which in 1958 he enshrined in the Scientific Policy Resolution for India — concepts which even today are relevant not only for India but to many other countries who are aspiring to benefit from the challenges contained in the process of science policy formulation.

P.J. Lavakare
J. George Waardenburg

REFERENCES

Blume, Stuart, Joske Bunders, Loet Leydesdorff and Richard Whitley (eds), 'The Social Direction of the Public Sciences', *Sociology of the Sciences Yearbook 1987*, D. Reidel, Dordrecht, 1987.

Chakravarty, Sukhamoy, *The Logic of Investment Planning*, North-Holland, Amsterdam, 1958.

—— *Development Planning: The Indian Experience*, Oxford University Press, Oxford, Delhi, etc., 1987.

Gibbons, Michael and Philip Gummett (eds), *Science, Technology and Society Today*, Manchester University Press, Manchester, 1984.

Gibbons, Michael, Philip Gummett and B.M. Udgaonkar (eds), *Science, and Technology Policy in the 1980s and Beyond*, Longman, London and New York, 1984.

Irvine, John and Ben R. Martin, *Foresight in Science: Picking the Winners*, Frances Pinter, London and Dover, NH, 1984.

Snellen, I.T.M., 'Social Merit as a Criterion of Scientific Choice: Its Application in Dutch Science Policy', *Minerva*, XXI, Spring, 1983.

Tinbergen, J., *The Theory of Economic Policy*, North-Holland, Amsterdam, 1952.

Part I: Science policy and national goals

Neither the existence of national goals, nor their way of coming into being, is obvious or unambiguous. Moreover, in whichever context and formulation national goals are expressed, the way they function in a large 'developing' socialist society, where planning is an accepted activity, could be quite different from that in a small 'developed' society with a mixed economy where a planning bureau has a strongly technical, mainly forecasting, task. A science policy will be developed within the framework of national goals, and therefore one would expect it to depend on the nature and functioning of these national goals.

Yet, surprisingly, it turns out that a meaningful intellectual discourse can exist on the subject of science policy and national goals even between persons from countries in several respects so different as India and The Netherlands, and even when it is focused primarily on their countries' experience. Diverse experience introduces a lively and instructive contrast between the situations within which common questions have to be answered, both theoretically and practically.

Some of such common issues may be expressed in the following questions. How is the relationship seen between science and national goals, as against general societal needs? How can science serve national goals better? How broadly (pure science excluded?) and how specifically should research priorities be formulated to that end? How is a synthesis conceivable between nationally decided R & D priorities and the spontaneous development of science? How is investment in R & D weighted against direct investment in economic development? How is domestic development of R & D regarded as opposed to adaptation of foreign R & D results and on which grounds does one select R & D areas for domestic development or for the adaptation of foreign results?

Some of these questions and others were put before the authors of the chapters; Dr S.R. Valluri chose to answer them quite precisely in his chapter on the Indian experience, while Professor S.S. Blume treats the issues more broadly in relation to the literature and to his experience in The Netherlands and elsewhere in Europe. Dr Ashok Jain was asked to enlarge his comments in the discussion for a special contribution on the issues of picking up signals for science policy from national government policy documents and of the need for accommodation of science policy vis-à-vis other policy areas.

1 A view from The Netherlands

Stuart Blume

INTRODUCTION: SOME GENERAL NOTIONS RELATING TO SCIENCE POLICY

The idea that research has important economic effects is far from new: it was recognized in the nineteenth century. But its significance for government policy — the idea that for economic reasons there should *be* a government policy towards research (and technology) — really only dates from the 1950s. At that time economists began to try to explain quantitatively the sources of economic growth (particularly in the United States). There seemed reasons to believe that advancing knowledge — identified with research — had played an important role in national growth. Economists such as Nelson began to set out the arguments for a major government role in the financing of research, pointing out that even in the richest nations industry would tend to underinvest in research. In more recent times the arguments surrounding investment in research, the rationale for government involvement, have evolved significantly. It is worth referring to three important intellectual developments.

First, the discussion associated with the Brooks Report of 1971 led to a significant broadening in the range of policy objectives to which research was supposed to contribute (OECD, 1971). The Brooks committee, established by the OECD, argued that research had to be mobilized in the interests of social objectives beyond the purely economic. Not only the search for economic growth, but also national objectives in areas like health, environment and housing should be made central to national research policy. This report proved of great significance in shifting the debate regarding science policy.

Second, the relations between research and its applications came to be looked at rather differently. The early studies of national economic growth had looked for a simple correlation between investment in research (R & D) and growth. It came increasingly to be recognized that R & D, however well performed, did not lead *inevitably* to new technology and wealth. Much depended on organization, on management, and on interorganizational connections. Studies in science policy and innovation were now exploring the factors — like organization — which mediated the relationship between R & D and application. Under what conditions does investment in research pay off? Why was it that some countries, or some firms, spent a lot of money on R & D and seemed to get little concrete benefit for their investments? Were they spending money on the wrong R & D (as an influential Brookings study of the United Kingdom argued in the 1960s), or were the problems ones of institutional links? This development typically had negative consequences for the social sciences. Not only was the fact that social science research is typically useful in rather different ways from the natural sciences forgotten, but it was unthinkingly assumed that the same forms of research organization would be optimum for these disciplines too (Bulmer, 1982).

Third, in the past few years, there has emerged a sense that certain strategic sectors could provide Western countries with a way out of the recession in which they found themselves from the mid-1970s. In one country after another reports identifying biotechnology, microelectronics, information science, new materials, etc. as the crucial sectors appeared. These fields had to be funded lavishly, it was argued, freed from the constraints on investment in R & D which had tended to develop in the 1970s (Rothwell and Zegveld, 1981). As a result policymakers began to interest themselves in newly developing fields like these. More gradually, an interest in developing methods for identifying emergent fields with the same 'strategic' potential has also arisen.

This faith in science and technology is not limited to the rich West. The general beliefs underlying the Indian government's Technology Policy Statement of 1983 were probably shared by most Western governments:

The base of science and technology consists of trained and skilled manpower at various levels, covering a wide range of disciplines, and an appropriate institutional, legal and fiscal infrastructure. Consolidation of the existing scientific base and selective strengthening of thrust areas in it are essential. Special attention will be given to the promotion and strengthening of the technology base in newly emerging and frontier areas such as information and materials science, electronics and biotechnology.

DERIVING PRIORITIES FOR SCIENCE POLICY FROM NATIONAL GOALS

Many of the current priorities for S & T policy derive from a general international consensus that biotechnology, microelectronics, etc. are the key sectors in the 1980s. They were identified in the first place by committees of scientists and technologists looking for areas of technological opportunity (see Rothwell and Zegveld, 1981; Irvine and Martin 1984). The attempt to establish future areas of strategic opportunity, whether using panels of experts (as in Delphi-methods for example) or using bibliometric tools is still attracting a good deal of interest today. But it must be recognized that this relates to opportunities offered (or thought to be offered) by the 'state of the art' in science. It is an approach which takes no account either of possibilities of capitalizing on these opportunities, or of specific national needs. In other words, priorities of this kind did not derive from the attempt to establish research priorities explicitly on the basis of national social and economic goals. More comprehensive exercises which have tried to develop research priorities on that basis have been attempted, though with mixed results.

At the beginning of the 1980s Unesco initiated one of the most comprehensive attempts at deriving priorities for science from national goals that there has been. On the basis of a carefully elaborated formal method (Unesco, 1977), a number of countries — including Argentina, Australia, Costa Rica, Jordan and Portugal — set about formal development of science policy priorities. The method entailed three steps (i) generation, prioritization and interrelation of national development goals; (ii) interrelating of fields of knowledge relevant to such goals, whether directly or indirectly; (iii) assessment of the interrelations between goals and fields of knowledge, in order to establish the 'relevance' of each field of knowledge and thereby indicate priorities. The process required those carrying out the exercise (groups of scientists and of policymakers) to start with official documents setting out the government's priorities regarding national goals — where these exist. Generally speaking these embody the relatively short time span of political action, so that they have in some way to be extended. Science and technology do not yield their fruits within the lifetime of the average elected government. Moreover the goals had to be specific enough for implications for research to be derived from them. This was mostly not the case: national goals are often couched in very general terms (for example: 'better health for all'), reflecting the political/integrative function which they sometimes have. This is especially so of goals relating to social or cultural development. It is very difficult to translate government commitment to 'equality of opportunity', or 'freedom of expression' or 'enhanced scope for regional cultural development' into precise operational goals with time scales attached. As I pointed out in a review of the Unesco method, this had important implications. It implied that the science policy analyst had to interrelate, prioritize, extend and articulate national goals as announced in political documents. The exercise was most feasible under certain conditions: for example where there is

a multi-year development plan, in which goals are treated as specific policy: technical things to be attained through specific steps. They will be least [possible] where goals are no more than implicit in policy, or where they take an essentially symbolic form . . . Much of the vocabulary of politics reflects the symbolic function of national goals: the attainment of 'independence' or 'self-reliance' or the 'just society' or 'equality'. The translation of such aspirations into practical goals is the very essence of politics and is *essentially* controversial. [Blume, 1983]

The practical experience of countries attempting the exercise was precisely that the generation of a list of national goals in a form in which science priorities could be deduced from them and then interrelated was conceptually and politically difficult. Who had the authority, power or political legitimacy to extrapolate and prioritize the national goals set out by National Planning Councils or suchlike? Inevitably politicians and administrators see great dangers in any such prioritization process, for its implication is that the policies or programmes of some ministries or agencies come to be more important than those of others. Moreover, setting out these goals in the form of specific targets with timescales attached obviously makes progress or lack of progress very clear indeed to political opponents! There was thus an inbuilt tension between the technical requirement or the priority setting and the need for political legitimacy for the exercise. There are conceptual difficulties also. How do we translate a goal such as 'better health for all' into priorities for science and technology? Even if we focus on a very specific aspect, like the health of newborn babies, this can be translated for research purposes in all kinds of ways, ranging from epidemiological studies (relative prevalence of different causes of disease and mortality or social correlates of disease) to microbiological research, nutritional studies, to economic studies, sociological or anthropological studies and so on. The same is true of many *operational* policy objectives. In practice, the research programmes that do generally emerge often reflect which scientific disciplines were represented in the decisionmaking.

This experience seems to imply that clear limits exist to the possibilities of deriving priorities for science from national goals in an unambiguous and purely formal manner; leaving aside that while it may be possible to speak unambiguously of 'national goals' in relation to countries with a tradition of national planning (like India), it is somewhat problematic to do so in relation to countries (like The Netherlands) in which the market plays a dominant role.

That there is no logical relationship of derivation does not mean that national priorities (in whatever form they exist) cannot be an important input to the establishment of priorities for science. The question then becomes that of establishing in what ways national goals can be a significant input to establishing priorities for R & D. That leads us to consider the social processes by which priorities for the research and development system are set in practice.

SOCIAL PROCESSES OF DECISIONMAKING IN SCIENCE POLICY

Experiences with the Unesco method of priority setting are only a small part of the evidence which has accumulated and which attests to the importance of the processes by which decisions are reached — and priorities set — in and for science. Many experts would agree that it is these processes — the nature of the consultations taking place between those making S & T policy and the researchers who would have to implement it — that are crucial to effective science policy. In Western countries these processes have changed quite a lot in the past ten to twenty years.

In the 1960s the scientific community enjoyed an unprecedented autonomy in its control over the resources the state chose to make available for science. Governments largely took the view that the scientific community could best decide where opportunities were to be sought. We might speak of the 'bottom up' establishment of priorities for science. Subsequently this came to be balanced by a 'top down' component, as governments began to make their own preferences felt. The 1970s were a period in which many governments took the view that they and their advisers could best decide how public funds for science should be spent (Blume, 1985). At the same time this 'top down' component in decisionmaking was becoming more complicated, reflecting developments in political culture. Who should represent the national interest in debate over scientific priorities? Must a regional element be introduced? We see priorities starting to be set in committees carefully constituted to represent the various interests in a given area of research: including representatives of science, users, regulation and so on.

In the last few years, and to varying extents, the formulation of priorities has come to be based upon broader patterns of consultation within and beyond the scientific community. There is evidence from Japan and elsewhere that broad consultation rather than hierarchical decisionmaking is appropriate to R & D. In the absence of such consultation processes there is the real danger that priorities established in committees may fail to influence the actual research priorities of the scientific community. There are examples of scientific groups happily accepting the funds attached to new priorities without doing more than 'relabelling' their ongoing research. There are examples of their failing even to apply for the funds, being wholly uninterested in the proposed research initiative! Such consultations can be more or less formalized. At one extreme would be the organization of workshops at which priorities in a field might be worked out. Another possibility is the establishment of permanent but informal networks. Slightly more formal, but comparable, is the example of the Sector Councils in The Netherlands. Here a broadly constituted group (representing all major interests in a field like agricultural research or health research) have the task of formulating broad indicative priorities for their field, taking into account the goals of the various social groups and the R & D plans of private research organizations (Snellen, 1983).

Despite recent interest in formal methods of assessment or priority setting, practical experience over the years shows the importance of the organizational structures within which priorities are set. Recent science policy analysis supports the instinct of many policymakers to the effect that the *right priorities are those which emerge from a properly constituted committee or other forum or process, in which the commitment of the scientific community gradually develops.* The crucial thing is then design of this forum or process.

Establishing national priorities for research is one thing. Especially where the scientific community is not deeply involved in the process of priority setting, implementing them may be quite another. Clearly the process of implementation is highly dependent upon the kind of relationship which the government (or individual priority-setting body) enjoys with the scientific community.

STIMULATING PRIORITY FIELDS

Given the growing concern, in almost all countries, in stimulating fields of science and technology deemed to offer particular national (economic or social) opportunity, a common question arises. How can this be done?

The process can be viewed as composed of a number of analytically distinct sub-processes (Rip Hagendijk and Dits, 1986)

- the **generation** of a priority (putting a potential priority on the agenda);
- the **articulation** of the priority (specification of approaches or solutions, further structuring of the goal);
- the **selection** of the priority: i.e. authoritative (political) endorsement of the priority;
- the **implementation** of the priority;
- **realization**, in the sense of performing the research required;
- the **evaluation** of outputs and outcomes.

Analysis of the total process, on the basis of empirical studies of successful and less successful implementation of priorities in Dutch science, suggested in the first place that implementation and articulation of priorities are intimately linked. In other words, there is a very important connection between the sub-process of deciding what kind of research exactly will be needed, what approaches are to be preferred and so on, and the sub-process of actually choosing researchers and negotiating their involvement in the new programme. The analysis also makes clear just how important getting — and retaining — the commitment of the scientific community can be.

Two kinds of implementation strategy are distinguished in this work, and each can be successful under certain circumstances. One is called an 'orchestration' strategy. This implies the policymaker taking his goals as the starting point and then being 'active in the selection of research and research institutions, in stimulating actors to do what he wants and in creating commitments'. The second strategy is termed 'accommodation': it implies trying only to bring about some modification of the existing state of affairs. Choice of one or the other should generally depend on the state of the research field in question. Rip *et al.* point out that strategies of accommodation are generally followed where fundamental research with long-term relevance is intended, while the more interventionist strategy is generally used where more immediate 'missions' are involved. The important thing is that different sorts of intellectual, social and organizational circumstances demand different sorts of implementation strategies. This seems to be true even within one European country, and reflects not only the important differences which exist between the various areas of science and technology, but also the diverse nature of national S & T priorities. Looked at from a broader international context, it seems possible that the political culture of a country, its preferred style of decisionmaking, will incline it towards one or other of these approaches to implementation. Problems of implementation, deriving from a mismatch between the nature of a given research priority and the style of implementation, thus will not be everywhere the same.

BUILDING UP CAPACITY

The effective domestic implementation of a research priority logically implies that appropriate institutions and expertise exist. Sometimes priorities may have this as their explicit objective: for example, building up a national competence in materials science or biotechnology (through postgraduate training and research programmes) may *itself* be the principal goal. Creating an institutional and manpower capacity is always an important element in policy directed towards new fields of science. There are two elements to this question of building up capacity as part of a priority programme: manpower and institutional. The institutional questions are complicated. Where should research expertise in the new field be built up? Under what circumstances is it advisable to set up a new organizational entity, or a new university department? Clearly, they are the questions discussed above under implementation strategy, and we have given some hints regarding them. If one looks at the history of the universities in the West, one finds that a number of new fields have been introduced in the first place because of a social need for skilled manpower (or woman power!), with research activity following along behind. This is especially true in fields relating to health and social service provision. In other areas the process has been the other way round. As research has come to be seen as important for the economy or society, the question has arisen of how results and competence can be diffused among the relevant social and economic organizations. It is now widely believed that the best way of transferring competence is by transferring people (see for example OECD, 1984), so trained people have to be produced by the academic system. Although few in Western Europe now believe in comprehensive manpower planning in the way that they did twenty years ago, there is a general view than manpower targets must be met in relation to priority fields like biotechnology and informatics. Sometimes these targets are based on a concept of economic demand (the number of specialists whom the economy will absorb: i.e., make paid employment for); sometimes they are based on a concept of 'national need'. A policy process which deduces a necessary level of research activity in a given field (say pharmacology or polymer science) from national goals and then asks 'how many scientists do we need to carry out this level of research?' produces a need-derived manpower target for the field. There is no certainty that these specialists, if trained, will find paid work.

LIMITATIONS ON THE POSSIBILITIES OF STEERING

What are the ultimate possibilities of science policy in a democratic country carrying out a relatively small share of the world's science? This is a problem shared by both India and The Netherlands, for despite their difference in size, both participate in an enterprise where some 35 per cent of total production takes place in the USA.

This chapter has presented a number of the policy issues as they appear in the light of current experience and of science policy research. Many current priorities in the West reflect the attempt to assess areas of opportunity offered by the state of science and technology. Their relevance for actual policy must depend on an assessment of the individual nation's possibilities of capitalizing on these opportunities. The rational development of comprehensive science and technology priorities on the basis of national plans or statements of national goals is typically problematic. This is so partly for reasons relating to political processes and legitimacy, and partly for intellectual reasons relating to 'translations'. Because of this processes of priority setting have come to be seen as a matter requiring careful attention. Many experts now consider that priorities have to emerge from broad (through structure) consultation with the scientific (and technical) community, rather than from a hierarchical system.

The implementation of priorities can take place in a variety of ways: there are a number of available strategies (notably those denoted as 'orchestration' and 'accommodation'). Which will work best depends on the nature of the field of science and the nature of the priority. Since the effective implementation of priorities often requires the build up of competence in the form of trained manpower, as well as the diffusion of this competence, the relations of S & T priorities with the higher education system (and provision of training programmes) is crucial and will need to be considered.

Though there is much to be done in the way of harnessing the science and technology system to national needs, possibilities are still limited. Capacity can be built up, work can be initiated and steps can be taken to ensure effective utilization of results. But in many fields disciplinary priorities also exist — emerging from an international disciplinary community in which the United States may well have a dominant position. Among the essentials for science policy today are a better understanding of its own limits and possibilities. This relates to the nature of the tools available, appreciation of the differences between the sciences in what research entails and understanding of the significance of the organizational context within which research takes place. Motivation of the scientific community, its commitment to the goals which the policy community wishes to see addressed, is then crucial. There is no substitute for commitment and motivation. That is part of the reason for which processes of priority setting are now of such great importance.

REFERENCES

Blume, S.S., 'Determining priorities for science and technology: a review of the Unesco method and its application', Unesco document S-83/CONF.731/2, September 1983.
——— The development of Dutch science policy in international perspective 1965–1985, RAWB Achtergrondstudies #14, The Hague, 1986.
Bulmer, M., The Uses of Social Research, Allen & Unwin, London, 1982.
Irvine, J. and B.R. Martin, Foresight in Science, Pinter, London, 1984.
OECD, Science, Growth and Society, OECD, Paris, 1971.
OECD, Industry and University, OECD, Paris, 1984.
Rip, A., R.H. Hagendijk and H. Dits, 'Processes of implementation of science policy priorities', unpublished paper based on Dutch-language RAWB publication, Amsterdam, September 1986.
Rothwell, R. and W. Zegveld, Industrial Innovation and Public Policy, Pinter, London, 1981.

Snellen, I.T.M., 'Social merit as a criterion of scientific choice: its application in Dutch science policy', *Minerva*, **XXI**, 1983, 16–36.

Unesco, *Method for Priority Determination in Science and Technology*, Science policy studies and documents #40, 1977.

2 A view from India

S.R. Valluri

INTRODUCTION

As an independent nation with control over its destiny, India is about four decades old. The industrial revolution which was backed up in later stages with large inputs from science and which transformed the Western world passed it by. Conscious efforts to use science and its offspring modern technology to improve the standards of living of the people were made with the start of the First Five-Year Plan of the government of India, in 1951. The idea that planned research can have important economic effects was explicitly recognized in the Indian context with the formal introduction of the national planning process. India has been attempting, during the last four decades, to bridge the science and technology gaps that had developed over the years. Forty years is not too long a time to bridge such wide gaps. In a country where a sizeable majority of people go to bed hungry every night and where amenities, treated as minimum necessities of life in the developed world, are considered luxuries, we are still feeling our way through and trying to use the planning process as the quickest and most economical way of 'bridging the gap'.

The problem is inherently complex. National Independence in 1947 raised large expectations from the people. Satisfying the minimum necessities of people by way of food, potable water and shelter continue to have a high priority. How complex the problem is can be seen when it is recognized that during the last forty years, the country's population increased from something like 300 million people to about 800 million currently spread over more than half a million villages. It has, however, become an article of faith that improvements in the standards of living can be obtained only through massive industrialization which, in recent times, has been backed to a considerable extent by developments in science, and science-based technologies in the Western world.

The Scientific Policy Resolution (SPR) of 1958[1] of the government of India was expected to become the guidepost for the planning process through the five-year plans. The directives contained in the Technology Policy Statements,[2] although explicitly framed only in 1983, were also implicitly assumed to be the guidelines from about the same time as the SPR. The planning process was expected to convert these various policies into programmes that could be implemented through the five-year plans. Looking back, it has to be concluded that although much has been achieved, there are still wide gaps. Expectations have far exceeded the achievements and resources. But the belief in science and technology as the essential ingredients for rapid improvement in living standards has been, if anything, reinforced over the years in spite of the fact there there were many hurdles to the implementation of the priorities in the spirit in which they were conceived.

The SPR passed by the Parliament more than thirty years ago stated:

The key to national prosperity apart from the spirit of the people, lies, in the modern age, in the effective combination of three factors, technology, raw materials and capital of which the first is perhaps the most important, since the creation and adoption of new scientific techniques can, in fact, make up for deficiency in natural resources, and reduce the demands on capital. But technology can only grow out of the study of science and its applications.

It is clear from the above that the SPR looks upon science as means to an end and not an end in itself. The end purpose would be the use of scientific knowledge to develop technology which would help to provide higher material standards of living for people.

The government headed by Jawaharlal Nehru, India's first prime minister, thus expressed implicit faith in the use of science to obtain material well-being for the Indian people. This demanded a build up of infrastructure for science through an enhanced university educational system (from about thirty universities in 1950 to about 160 now) and research laboratories (from a handful to about 1,700, of which about 900 are funded by the government and the balance by private industry). Nehru called these the temples of modern India. It would seem that his government also clearly recognized that it would take a very long time to transform the industrial base of India if this infrastructure alone and what it could deliver were to be the instruments for transformation. Therefore the government also concurrently set up a large public sector for heavy industry and encouraged the establishment of a private sector to respond to consumer needs. Both were mostly based upon imported 'know-how' for producing goods. It was apparently hoped that at some stage, the industry so established would start interacting with the R & D and the academic system. The expectation was that each would transform the other, the changing requirements of the country setting the pace, each element serving as the driving force for the other, increasing self-reliance and establishing a self-generating technology base as the years went by.

Maybe four decades is not sufficient to obtain such a transformation for a country like India. It would seem that dependence on imported technologies has not been significantly reduced, if anything, it may have increased. While there may be some exceptions, with a view to obtaining the latest technologies much of industry (whether private or public) liberally imports production 'know-how' for manufacture of goods. There would appear to be a tacit recognition of this 'need' by the government, although the official policy of self-reliance remains unchanged. What this liberal licensing has done is to reduce the incentive for increased self-reliance, particularly in advanced high-technology areas. Self-reliance became a casualty to expediency in a democracy subjected to diverse political pressures from various lobbies.

Lest there should be any doubts about the ability of the scientific/industrial community to rise to the occasion, one need only recall India's space and atomic energy programmes as evidence of such capability. When the government was clear about its priorities, and where it was difficult to obtain technologies from abroad, the Indian professional community rose to the occasion. The failure to obtain a greater degree of self-reliance in other fields would seem to be due to a mismatch between policies and operational priorities.

Mrs Indira Gandhi, the former prime minister, as long ago as 1970, in her inaugural address to the Third Round Table Conference of Scientists and Technologists in India put it succinctly when she said that the SPR was an expression of the aspirations of the people and not a blueprint for action. Action required that the philosophical foundations outlined in the SPR should be given shape through concrete programmes. Setting up an infrastructure for science through the university and research laboratory system, largely funded by government agencies, was not found to be very difficult, but to make the system interact with the industrial base to obtain a self-generating technology base turned out to be a different matter.

With some exceptions, the Indian industrial sector, whether private or public, does not seem to have generally recognized that R & D is means to an end and not an end in itself, and that R & D is a part of the invention/innovation chain, its output becoming a purposeful input to the industry only if the industry desires it to be so and only if the government formulates policies that are conducive to such interaction, and helps in establishing purposeful linkages. In an environment where it is easy to import production 'know-how' for goods selling in a seller's market, there was no incentive for the Indian industrialist to stake his future on indigenously developed technologies which have not been sufficiently tested and proven. In essence, while the liberal licensing policy in the name of importing latest technologies may be helping the establishment of a production base, in the absence of an incentive or a driving force for its absorption, growth of self-reliance most certainly did not receive the kind of support it deserved, considering that it is the avowed policy of the government. Thus, the question raised by Blume[3] in his chapter is equally relevant in the Indian context. 'Under what conditions does investment in research pay off? Why was it that some countries, or some firms, spent a lot of money on R & D and seemed to get little concrete benefit for their investments? Were they spending money on the wrong R & D or were the problems one of institutional links? To add one more parameter: is it that governments tend to hold their basic policies in abeyance to respond to political pressures? Is it that the changing perceptions of the administrators greatly influence the decisions which are designed to implement policy, particularly if the policy objectives are in the nature of lofty ideals, or liable to distortion in implementation? The primary driving force to do things by ourselves can then get subordinated to the easier and economically less risky alternative of production under licence. In this background the soft option of licence production in the name of importing the latest technologies became an operational virtue.

We have to recognize that, for developing countries like India which are trying rapidly to transform their economies, fairly large licence production, in response to urgent consumer needs, is inevitable for the near future. Wisdom seems to lie in their selective absorption using them to build an indigenous technology base in contrast to an industrial base which simply produces goods. This seems to be the practical alternative as time is not on our side. The trouble seems to come in the absorption stage and building on it. It is difficult. But it is only on such a foundation that a country can establish a base for self-generating technologies. The temptation to obtain one more licence for a more recent product (even if it were already obsolete in the country of its origin) is much too tempting in an economy that operates in a seller's market. The easy availability of licences for the next generation product reduces risk and the need to absorb technology. Absorption of technology involves not simply reading production drawings and understanding specifications, but understanding the underlining scientific, technological and design principles which would enable the use of such knowledge to develop a better product indigenously.

It may be noted that no country is so self-reliant that it does not need to buy any technologies from others. It would seem that for us wisdom lies in increasing our technology base to a level where what we pay for buying technologies can to a reasonable extent be compensated by what we sell to others. The bottom line for buying and selling technologies should eventually balance out which is, in fact, the case for most developed countries. The current talk of complete self-reliance at any cost, which would be tantamount to self-sufficiency, has no meaning in the Indian context.

There is one more parameter to be considered in this context. Science does not stand still. Unless as a nation we start investing money and pay attention to emerging technologies such as biotechnology, microelectronics, artificial intelligence, etc., we are likely to be caught up in the vicious circle of forever trying to catch up with the developed world. So the reference points are two-fold if increasing self-reliance is our objective: first to bridge selectively the gaps that have already developed over the years; and second, to start research concurrently in at least some of the emerging areas, as they are developing elsewhere in the world. Our problem is more difficult, particularly with limited financial resources. We need, however, to keep at least a low-profile activity in emerging areas to keep ourselves abreast of development elsewhere, while closing the gaps in sciences and technologies that are already existing in crucial areas.

Our SPR was reviewed by a high-level committee of the government around the same time this committee was shaping the Technology Policy Statement. It came to the conclusion that twenty-five years after it was approved by our Parliament SPR had not lost its basic relevance and continued to be valid. This is not really surprising. In a sense it is a philosophical document, and a general guideline to evolve programmes for implementation. The principles to which it subscribes, and which are mentioned as aims, seem to be equally valid for any country that would like to subscribe to the scientific methodology for pursuit of knowledge and apply it to improve living standards. In regard to its implementation, it is clear that our forward-looking basic research, which can offer scientific and technological breakthroughs, must be contemporary with what is going on elsewhere in the world. It is this concern, more than anything else, that prompts the government of India to look into fields like biotechnology, microelectronics, superconductivity etc. It is also equally clear that we need a shift in emphasis in licensing policies, if R & D is to play a more active role in increasing self-reliance. This problem of bridging gaps selectively while keeping ourselves abreast of the emerging technologies which have relevance to us is what prioritization in the planning process is about. We do not yet seem to have rationally agreed solutions to this complex problem. We are feeling our way through.

TECHNOLOGY POLICY AS A DERIVATIVE FROM THE POLICY FOR SCIENCE

Our science policy cannot be really discussed without referring to our Technology Policy Statement issued in 1983. It stated:

Our philosophy of a mixed economy involves the operation of the private, public and joint sectors, including those with foreign equity participation. . . . Directives must clearly define systems for the choice of technology, taking into account economic, social and cultural factors along with technical considerations; indigenous development and support to technology, and utilisation of such technology; acquisition of technology through import and its subsequent absorption, adaptation and upgradation; ensuring competitiveness at international levels in all necessary areas; and establishing links between the various elements concerned with generation of technology, its transformation into economically utilisable form, the sector responsible for production (which is the user of such technology), financial institutions concerned with resources needed for these activities and the promotional and regulating arms of the government.

These directives demand well thought out procedures for their implementation. The pace for achievement of self-reliance depends very much on the relative priorities proposed to be given to various parts of these directives and this in turn is largely influenced by political will as expressed through administrative decisions.

DIFFICULTIES IN DERIVING PRIORITIES

The extremely broad scope of the directives, which is perhaps what it should be at the national level, demands deriving specific priorities for science and technology. The directives outlined in TPS are not easy to implement. Perusal of plan documents issued by the government tend to indicate that planing for science and technology in India became overwhelmed by the need to give priority to sectors such as food production, power generation, health and sanitation, etc. where the problems were more down to earth with solutions generally known and only requiring adaptation and implementation. It would appear that India came to the same conclusion that Blume pointed out, i.e. that the generation of 'a list of national goals in a form in which science priorities could be deduced from them and then interrelated, was conceptually and politically difficult'. The result is that even the seventh five-year plan,[4] which followed the issuance of the TPS, does not seem to reflect the impact of this policy. For practical purposes, planning for S & T stands somewhat in isolation from the rest of the planning process.

IMPLICATIONS FOR PLANNING

The results are interesting. Where there is a particular department of the government whose activities are largely science/technology based, and where input–output linkages have been built up between the scientific research to be carried out and the expected technology development from it, the results have shown that a self-generating technology base could be established. The departments of space and atomic energy readily come to mind. They have been set up with specific objectives: the political will of the nation backed a scientific/technological objective, viz., the development of launch vehicles, satellites and nuclear power plants. In the green revolution which was ushered into the country through close interaction between the agricultural university system, agricultural research institutions and extension services, we had a similar success story. Food production increased from about 50 million tonnes at the time of Independence in 1947 to an anticipated 170 million tonnes by 1988. In other words where the articulation of a priority was specific, its implementation was fairly straightforward but not necessarily simple. It would seem that success was also assured, to a considerable extent, by the fact that implementation of these programmes was in the hands of professionally knowledgeable people who were aware of the consequences of their decisions. Self-reliance in some of these fields became a matter of necessity as it had not been found easy to import the relevant technologies, and there was political will backing the development of such technologies indigenously. It would seem that non-availability of technology from abroad acted as a strong driving force for the growth of an indigenous technology base.

INFLUENCE OF MARKET FORCES

However, the Indian experience also tended to indicate that where the market demand was potentially very high and the needs were urgent, licence production could hold an upper hand. This is so in spite of the infrastructure for a fairly good R & D base that has been established. Continued licence production in the garb of 'proven technology' prevented interaction between R & D and downstream users. The urgency to respond to immediate societal needs appears to have had a more decisive say in the final outcome than the long-term philosophical implications of the SPR. In virtually every case the argument between growth of self-reliance and licence production was settled by the market forces demanding quick solutions. Except in a few isolated instances, even the corporate R & D of the public sector, which was expected to be a pace-setter, turned out to be a trapping rather than a driving force for technology development of new products. Time was not on the side of those arguing in favour of implementing the avowed national policies. And, unfortunately for us, massive investments and sustained efforts are needed if any breakthroughs in science are to be converted to technological breakthroughs particularly in high-science–high-technology areas. In general we seem to start late, say after a paper appears in a journal, and continue with minimal investments until the equipment gathers dust. Each level of transition from basic research to applied research to technology development, and its application in the development of a new product and its manufacture, requires anywhere from a five to tenfold increase in investment. This aspect does not seem to have been appreciated in shaping and implementing our policy for increasing the pace of self-reliance. And perhaps what is even more serious is the fact that in some instances sophisticated hardware development programmes have been started without a prior technology development backup. As is well known, such a course of concurrent technology development is fraught with dangers. In the developed world, the science and technology base is substantially, if not fully, built before it forms an input into the development of a new product. The risks otherwise are too high. Long-term policies are required so that R & D is taken up, forming a desirable and deliberate input downstream for a hardware development project. There is no way R & D can respond suddenly in a competitive manner as an alternative to an imported licence production programme. It is unrealistic to think so. It is felt that the Indian experience is not unique, indeed is typical of developing countries in a worldwide community where some others are only too willing to sell their products or offer production under licence.

FUNCTIONING OF R & D INSTITUTIONS IN THE PREVAILING ENVIRONMENT

It is against this background that one has to assess the functioning of the scientific research institutions and their interaction with industry. Government-funded research and research in corporate R & D institutions have not seemed to have played the same role as they normally do in the developed world. The R & D in these countries tends to work on programmes which have potential for development of new products, many of which eventually lead to production. In the developing countries many of the successfully demonstrated scientific discoveries and laboratory-level technology development programmes have remained in the R & D institutions. The marginal inputs through various stages of development frequently resulted in obsolete technologies that could not hold their own in a competitive market environment. The gulf between demonstration and successful use in production was rarely bridged in many instances.

CONSEQUENCES FOR THE RELATIONSHIP BETWEEN SCIENCE AND
NATIONAL GOALS

It has not been possible to define material goals to focus sharply on the science and technology content and take the developments all the way to production since the planning generally lacked a long-term perspective. When John F. Kennedy gave a long-term policy commitment in 1960 for the United States to put a man on the moon before the end of that decade, over 500,000 institutions, big and small, participated in the programme. This brought in a quantum change in American high-science–high-technology capability. One has to search hard for such long-term commitments in the developing countries involving integration of R & D efforts and hardware development programmes. It would appear that investments in scientific research and technology development continue to be made by governments on the same premise on which they were started, i.e. the faith that something good will come out of them eventually, that they ought to be continued and that these are the overheads that society has to pay for in order to keep its future options open.

The first issue for discussion is: how is the relationship seen between science and national goals? Does part of science, the pure part, fall outside the national goals? Do the national goals and the societal needs for R & D coincide or should they be distinguished? For a country like India, with its tremendous diversity in living standards, it is difficult to define uniformly acceptable criteria for societal needs. To what extent R & D should be related to societal needs would therefore depend very much on the definition of national priorities in determining such needs. It is also dependent upon the ready availability of the relevant knowledge from elsewhere in the world. R & D on problems that would benefit the largest number of people in the country should clearly receive high priority. Allocations for R & D in agriculture, technology missions for drinking water, edible oils, etc. seem to indicate the government's concern to give priority to such problems. In other explicitly defined fields such as atomic energy and space, which may be considered national goals, the relationship between R & D and national goals has been quite specific. Such a relationship, however, does not seem to be evident in the R & D carried out by many of the other bodies, in the sense that the R & D programmes do not seem to have been derived from any national goals in any discernible manner. Considering that India is a developing country with limited resources, we cannot afford too much undirected research. We have to relate our R & D programmes, wherever possible, to societal needs. At the same time we have to recognize the freedom for academic institutions to take up open-ended and basic research even if unrelated to any clearly thought out national goals. At a time when today's basic research becomes tomorrow's applied research and may well lead to technology development the day after, this freedom of the academic institutions must be zealously guarded.

SOME RECENT ATTEMPTS TO RELATE SCIENCE AND NATIONAL GOALS:
ORCHESTRATION VERSUS ACCOMMODATION

A recent attempt to establish relevant linkages is the stipulation by the
government that autonomous R & D bodies like the Council of Scientific
and Industrial Research (CSIR) Laboratories should earn 30 per cent of
their expenditure through sponsored work. This demands a significant
shift in the emphasis of their research. While this stipulation is desirable,
it cannot ensure that purposeful interaction will take place between
industry and R & D. For purposeful interaction, the government should
simultaneously stipulate that the public sector should sponsor R & D
programmes in the academic institutions and research laboratories such
that a certain percentage of their sales (depending upon the nature of the
industry) would be used to absorb imported technologies and to develop
them further. Representatives from the R & D institutions must be
included in the boards of the public-sector undertakings and vice versa
to approve linkages at working level. For private industry, perhaps a rate
or tax equivalent to the licensing fees paid might be levied, with a
proportionate reduction if a research laboratory is set up to help absorb
the imported know-how or if R & D work is sponsored. Without such
stipulations, viable linkages cannot be built in the prevailing environment.

The formulation of thrust area programmes in the department of
science and technology of the government of India is another attempt to
make R & D in academic institutions and research laboratories respond
more directly to certain national objectives. This is a recent development
and it is too soon to draw conclusions. There has also been an attempt
in recent times to define a number of national 'technology missions'[5] to
which R & D is expected to contribute in a purposeful manner. These
are national goals and intended to respond to societal needs. As a result
of these developments, some changes may be expected in the functioning
of those R & D institutions that are not vertically integrated with the
downstream users. Successful implementation of programmes such as
technology missions really calls for an 'orchestration strategy' in which
every institution is assigned a task to be accomplished. Such an approach
is more a rule than an exception in the vertically integrated science-and-
technology-based agencies of the government in the sense that their
R & D programmes are mostly derived from the technology missions;
and on the basis of an overall plan, the programmes are orchestrated.
However, the structure and functioning of many of the R & D and
academic institutions are more amenable to an 'accommodation strategy'
in which, through sponsorship, the R & D activities of such institutions
are redirected. A sense of commitment and accountability is found more
in an orchestration strategy than in an accommodation strategy. It is not
easily possible to create a new department of the government under
which programmes can be vertically integrated and orchestrated every
time a need is perceived, unless such a programme has large political,
technological and financial implications. In the initial phases of growth
of R & D, infrastructure build-up tends to focus on open-ended and
forward-looking research. If purposeful linkages are not established fairly

soon, so that in due course such research could be reorientated towards more purposeful avenues, the functioning of such institutions loses relevance rapidly. These institutions become too accustomed to their freedom of operation and lack of accountability. Prudence demands that wherever possible we shift from 'accommodation mode' to 'orchestration mode' to obtain maximum return on investment in technology-orientated R & D.

HOW CAN SCIENCE BE MADE TO SERVE NATIONAL GOALS BETTER?

The second set of questions raised for discussion is: how can science be made to better serve national goals such as economic development, welfare, health, education, agriculture, industrialization? How can these goals be defined practically — that is in terms of scientific questions — in order that R & D can be geared to it? How specific should such priorities be (area, theme, programme, project)? Is it a top-down process or a bottom-up process? The difficulty which most planned economies face in answering such questions is that these words encompass so many things that a unique R & D programme cannot be easily derived out of such broad national goals. As we all know, science and technology deals with specifics and quantifiable things and national goals deal with more general subjects having emotional overtones in order to carry politically the largest number of people along. The crux of the problem is concretizing these goals. It is here that the interplay among the political/ administrative arm of the government, the economists who assess resource availability and define broad objectives and S & T people who have to examine the alternatives for implementation within stipulated time-scales and resources become important. We do not as yet seem to have any tried and tested ways of deriving the scientific objectives from sociological goals. Discussions among the interested parties under the auspices of our Planning Commission or some of the science departments such as the Department of Science and Technology, CSIR, the Indian Council for Agricultural Research (ICAR) etc. are avenues that are used to obtain some priorities among several alternatives. Generally speaking, capability to define explicit R & D programmes rests with the R & D institutions. However, the information and knowledge to define R & D programmes that will have the largest impact and national relevance may normally be expected to come from the Planning Commission and government departments. Unless there is compatibility between what R & D needs to be taken up and the ability to take up such R & D at the institutional level, mismatch between policies and programmes can arise leading to shortfalls in achievement of plan objectives. Common-sense therefore dictates that it should not be either a top-down or a bottom-up process. An iterative process of definition of programmes has the largest chance of success.

INDICATION OF NATIONAL GOALS AND R & D EFFORT

The third question raised is what indication do the national goals give with regard to the question: 'which R & D efforts must be made domestically and for which areas of knowledge must one rely on foreign results combined with domestic adaptation (for example in connection with self-reliance as a national goal)?' It will be recalled that India faces a dual problem: to fill the gaps in our technology and industrial bases as rapidly as possible through the import of 'know-why' as well as 'know-how' and to absorb and build on them; and second, to keep a watch on the emerging technologies in the developed world to examine their implications for us with a view to starting such activity here also. It cannot be said that India has so far been a leader in any emerging technologies. Generally speaking, it plays the role of a follower. Not that this is bad in itself since developments elsewhere in the world provide an opportunity for us to assess the pros and cons for taking up similar work in India. But then having started late, we have to put in much more effort to catch up with others. We are still operating in the first mode, i.e. net importers of technology. This is so in spite of the fairly wide R & D base that has been set up. One has to conclude that the research and technology development programmes may not have been properly conceived or adequately funded. The major constraints on the national goal of increasing self-reliance are time-scales and limited financial resources. These do not always permit indigenous R & D to evolve to a stage where production could be based upon it more economically in the short term as compared to setting up such production through licences. We take up basic and forward-looking applied research for one or two purposes: either that we have decided to proceed on our own as time is on our side and we cannot obtain such knowledge from others, and there are chances of obtaining breakthroughs within the country, or our knowledge of the underlying sciences and technologies in such fields will put us in a better bargaining position when the time comes to import such technologies. However the stated preference for import know-how for more production under licence for whatever reason inevitably leaves the national objective of increasing self-reliance in the back seat in this scenario. The problem is no longer one of making scientific choices but the difficult art of compromise among diverse groups with different perceptions operating in such a democratic setup with all its contradictions, but hopefully, while doing so, not sacrificing the objective of self-reliance. Not an easy problem, given the best of circumstances.

NATIONAL R & D PRIORITIES AND SPONTANEOUS DEVELOPMENT OF SCIENCE

The fourth question is: 'How does one conceive of the relation between R & D priorities, decided upon nationally, and the spontaneous development of science?' By their very nature, spontaneous developments in science are difficult if not impossible to orchestrate. What one can do at best is to create an environment and culture in which such spontaneous development in science can take place. When these show potential for exploitation, one would hope that such developments would obtain support in the form of national goals to exploit such breakthroughs for national benefit.

CHOICE BETWEEN INVESTMENT IN R & D AND ECONOMIC DEVELOPMENT

The fifth question for discussion is: 'how is the choice between investment in R & D and in economic development directly looked at?' In the Indian context the answer to this problem is in a sense self-evident. Government investments are proposed mostly to obtain immediate economic benefits. Such benefits are clearly a high-priority alternative to take us over the threshold of poverty to one of reasonable freedom from want for the majority of the people. However, it is also equally clear from even a cursory study of developed nations with better standards of living that it is not possible to become a part of this group without significant R & D investments.

The first priority of the nation is economic development and use of R & D knowledge from wherever it is available towards this end. Therefore production of goods under licence based upon imported know-how and using proven technologies seems to demand greater attention from the decisionmakers in spite of the basic commitment to growth of self-reliance. In a sense, it is therefore a miracle that India succeeded in increasing its investment in R & D close to the guideline percentage of 1 per cent of GNP proposed by UNESCO. This investment has to be looked upon as one of faith and an investment for future benefits.[6]

IMPLICATIONS OF STATISTICS FOR R & D INVESTMENT PATTERNS

It may be seen from DST statistics of 1986–7[6] that in the present-day world there is a very direct correlation between R & D investments and standards of living. Notwithstanding many limitations, international comparison throws some light on the inter-country differences in the resources deployed on R & D and standards of living. Most of the developed countries devote 2–3 per cent of their GNP to R & D. For developing countries this figure is marginal. For India this figure for 1986–7 was 1.03 per cent, having risen from about 0.23 per cent in 1958–9. Per capita R & D expenditure for India is US$2.78 (1986) whereas for most of the developed countries it is at least US$120.0. For The Netherlands these figures are 1.9 per cent (1980) and US$190.0 (1982) respectively. Being far behind, we may perhaps have to spend much more. These comparisons tend to indicate that for India, a substantial increase in inputs into R & D is needed to obtain the transformation from a developing to a developed country. In spite of the increase in investments in R & D during the last few decades, we do not yet seem to have crossed threshold investments to ensure visible benefits from R & D.

In trying to seek an answer to the basic question of investments in scientific research, I can do no better than quote the American nuclear physicist Alwin M. Weinberg. 'The cost of applied science will have to be treated as the overhead charges on the task it seeks to further; the cost of mission-oriented basic science to be the overhead charge on mission-oriented applied science and the purest science will have to be considered as an overhead for the entire technological system.'[7] It would seem that for India this is equally valid, subject to the proviso that the research for many of the problems for which we seek solutions has been already done elsewhere and it would be cheaper for India to adapt such knowledge and build on it instead of independently redeveloping it. The Indian R & D effort has in many cases yet to really establish itself as a techno-economically credible alternative in lieu of production know-how imports for manufacture of goods. Unfortunately we do not seem to have done well even in unravelling the underlying scientific, engineering and design principles and building on them to reduce further dependence on others for such knowledge.

TECHNOLOGY ASSESSMENT AND CHOICES

The sixth point is that of 'Technology assessment and problems of making choices between different technologies'. This is an important problem for us in view of the number of technologies we need to import to respond to immediate needs. Our ability to absorb a technology and build on it is dependent upon the level at which we can understand and develop such a technology ourselves if and when occasion demands. If the imported technology is too complex, it will stand in isolation from the technology fabric of society. If it is too simple, even if we gain time to respond to immediate needs, it will not help us in our movement towards greater self-reliance. These arguments lead us to the conclusion that we have to have adequate trained manpower well versed in a wide range of technologies and their future implications, even if we have no plans to develop them ourselves. Technology, if it is to be imported at all, is the prime concern of industry. Setting the pace for its absorption to increase self-reliance is the concern of the government. People with some knowledge of modern technologies (particularly advanced and emerging technologies) are most likely to be found in the academic and R & D institutions unless an industry is committed to R & D as an article of faith. Technology assessment, choice between various technologies and technology forecasting will therefore have to be evolved as a joint exercise among these institutions. Again, this is also an exercise in priorities requiring the build-up of competence in the form of trained manpower, as well as the diffusion of the competence and relating S & T priorities to the higher education system. At present, however, such interaction is not taking place effectively. It cannot be said that manpower in the academic institutions and research laboratories is involved in such tasks except through intermittent committee work. The result is that their work tends to lose relevance to the needs of the technology base which they have been set up to serve. Mobility as a means of transferring such knowledge from one institute to the other has not succeeded well owing to socio-economic reasons.

CONCLUSION

What little experience we have gained in our effort to implement the Scientific Policy Resolution and Technology Policy Statement with a view to increasing self-reliance tends to indicate that priority-setting from a set of alternatives is not amenable to any simplified procedures. We have to continue to depend upon imported technologies and while doing so, we have to have enough knowledge among the various bodies in the country to examine such imports from different angles and take action for their selective absorption among the R & D and production organizations in order to reduce external dependence and increase self-reliance at a faster pace.

We have to realize finally that applied research and developments in technology are means to ends and not ends in themselves. If they are to be purposeful, their sense of direction and pace must be set by the industry through an interactive dialogue with R & D laboratories and academic institutions. If industry does not take the initiative, precious little can be achieved by way of increasing self-reliance. Government, as the owner of the public sector which hopes to reach commanding heights of the economy, has an important role to play through its policy directives to create a dynamic partnership among academic institutions, R & D laboratories and industry.

NOTES

1. Scientific Policy Resolution, Government of India (1958).
2. Technology Policy Statement, Government of India (1983).
3. S.S. Blume, 'A view from The Netherlands' (Chapter 1 of this book).
4. *Seventh Five Year Plan 1985–90*, Vols 1 & 2, Planning Commission, Government of India (1985).
5. *Seventh Five Year Plan (1985–90)*, Vol. 2, p. 348 (1985).
6. *Research and Development Statistics 1986–87*, Department of Science & Technology, Government of India (1988).
7. Alvin M. Weinberg, *Minerva* I, 2 (Winter 1963) pp. 159–71.

3 Signals and regimes for science policy in India: some observations

Ashok Jain

INTRODUCTION

The concept of 'science policy' emerged out of the changing nature of scientific research requiring large investments and organized structures. The intimate relationship between research and technology development broadened the scope of science policy and often the term 'science and technology policy' came into usage in decisionmaking processes. The realization that science and technology contribute to national development has enhanced the importance of formulating and understanding policies for science and technology.

Decisionmaking takes place at various tiers, at the levels of research team, institution, organization or corporation, agency, etc. on to the national level. Science and technology policy consists of instruments that aid decisions on support, use, and regulation of science and technology at all levels. While science and technology policy has characteristic features addressing mainly issues relating to research and development, the decisionmaking process has to encompass other related areas such as industry, commerce, trade, health, welfare of the people and in general the development needs of society. A clear demarcation between regimes of science and technology policy and other policies is not possible. The higher the decision tier, the larger is the overlap between different policy regimes. Despite this non-separable and overlapping nature of different policy regimes, especially at the national level, nations do formulate policies and articulate policies for different sectors, including the science and technology sector. Structures for converting these policy statements into plans and programmes also exist. These policies and structures constitute modalities of state intervention in decisions relating to development of different sectors.

Many nations, including India, have specific policy statements on science and technology (S & T). In order to make these statements compatible with other policy regimes, S & T policies necessarily refer to aspects other than research and development. A common statement in R & D policy pronouncements is that science and technology is to be supported and used for national goals, implying thereby that while taking decisions on science and technology other policies that articulate national goals have to be taken note of. The Indian policy pronouncements contained in its Scientific Policy Resolution of 1958 and the Technology Policy Statement of 1983 are no exceptions. Should one, therefore expect derivation of specific policy instruments for science and technology down to the various levels of decisionmaking from S & T policy statements alone? An algorithm for deriving science and technology priorities from national level statements is difficult, more so at the institution level, and almost impossible down to the research team level. The national goals articulated in different policy statements, however, give strong signals to various structures responsible for the planning of activities in different sectors. In India, the role of policy statements in different regimes is to provide signals that establish a common perception of developmental issues resulting in a kind of integration of plans and programmes.

The capacity of Indian science and technology structures to pick up signals from other policy regimes has often been influenced by the perceptions of the political leadership of the extent and nature of overlap between the S & T policy regime and other regimes. A tendency to steer S & T policy in a distinct regime separable from other policy regimes also surfaces when those involved in decisionmaking on science and technology try to consolidate their constituency on the basis of actors who like to pick up signals solely from science and technology. The identification of a constituency becomes important for legitimation of decisions. The process of science and technology policy formulation and its implementation is, therefore, more in the nature of accommodation and adjustment between various constituencies rather than orchestration, with political leadership playing an important role. Orchestration is all the more difficult in the Indian context of a mixed economy (public and private sector co-existing) working within the framework of a democratic socialist republic.

Developments in Indian science and technology policy can, therefore, be understood by looking at (a) the type of signals that are generated by different policy regimes and how these signals are picked up by institutions and actors involved in science and technology policy formulation at various tiers of decisionmaking; (b) perceptions regarding overlap between different regimes; and (c) the constituencies generated for legitimation purposes.

SIGNALS FROM NATIONAL GOALS

(i) The structures set up for scientific research after independence in 1947 derived their research areas from the goals of national development contained in the apex policy document, the Constitution of India. The directive principles contained in the constitution required that the management and ownership of national resources be for the benefit of the population at large. This meant that research and development activities for exploration and exploitation of national resources had to be set up within the government institutions. The Council of Scientific and Industrial Research (CSIR) picked up this signal and became the prime agent for research and development on coal, ocean resources and minerals. Similarly oil and natural gas resources became the responsibility of the government research institutions.

(ii) Another example of science and technology priorities derived directly from national goals are the programmes of research institutions for solving problems of small-scale industries. The government had set a goal for encouraging small- and medium-scale industries as part of its industrial policy and this sent signals to the CSIR system. Research and development projects at its laboratories made significant contributions to the development of small-scale industries.

(iii) During the sixties, the Industrial Policy Resolution and the Industry Act gave a list of items in which import of technology was not allowed. This list was interpreted by the research system as 'import substitution', a term that gave it a clear direction for priority setting. This industrial policy instrument combined with the Indian Patent Act of 1970 resulted in a large number of indigenous technologies in chemicals, pharmaceuticals, fertilizers, electronics, etc. going into production.

One can add a number of other examples to illustrate how at the organization level (CSIR) and the institution level (laboratories of CSIR) signals were picked up from policy announcements on national goals and instruments used for industrial development. These signals were no doubt compatible with the Scientific Policy Resolution of 1958 which said that science must benefit the people.

ACCOMMODATION PROCESS BETWEEN DIFFERENT POLICY REGIMES

Although there are only two main policy statements often quoted in relation to Indian Science and Technology — the Scientific Policy Resolution of 1958 and the Technology Policy Statement of 1983 — we have seen how policies in other sectors influence the decisionmaking process in science and technology. The exchange of signals between the science and technology policy regime and other regimes has been strongly influenced by the perception of the political leadership and of science and technology decisionmakers on the nature and extent of overlap between different regimes. These perceptions form constituencies of decisionmakers that are willing to effect adjustment and accommodation by accepting or ignoring signals from different policy regimes.

Until the seventies, decisionmaking in science and technology was essentially within a strong constituency consisting of the scientific elite and political leadership. The research infrastructure consisting of a chain of laboratories under the Council of Scientific and Industrial Research (CSIR), the Department of Atomic Energy (DAE), the Indian Council of Agricultural Research (ICAR), the Defence Research and Development Organization (DRDO), etc. derived their policy orientations essentially from the S & T policy regime perceived by this constituency. In the case of industrial and agricultural research, signals from other policy regimes were difficult to ignore. CSIR and ICAR picked up those signals from the socio-economic sectors that did not call for significant restructuring of their position with the science and technology constituency and consequently required least accommodation. A need for setting up mechanisms or structures that would accept overlap between the S & T policy regime and the policy regimes of the other sectors was not felt. Decisionmaking in science and technology under its strong constituency was quick; accommodation was never a serious problem. The growth of research infrastructure in this ethos was rapid and extensive.

The situation started changing in the seventies. The less-than-expected progress in the socio-economic sectors, problems of foreign exchange and several other factors brought into focus the question of direct utilization of research and infrastructure for solving the developmental problems. This was also the period when environmental concerns and social assessment of science and technology had become important issues in the Western countries. This led to the formulation of the first S & T Plan in 1975 with R & D programmes formulated in the context of goals for economic and social sectors as defined by the sixth five-year plan prepared by the Planning Commission of the government of India. This meant a formal recognition of an overlap of the policy regime of science and technology with other regimes. A process of setting up of structures for planning science and technology that would incorporate signals from other sectors was initiated with an expectation of 'orchestration'. It is interesting to note that the S & T constituency, used to accommodation within itself, found itself confronted with the need for orchestration of programmes formulated and implemented under a much wider constituency. That was not easy and indeed the structures did not work.

THE CHANGING CONSTITUENCIES AND TENSIONS

The process started in 1975, however, has continued. What has evolved is not the setting up of algorithms for rationally deriving S & T priorities from national goals, but stronger demands that S & T integrate with socio-economic plans. At the planning level, the programmes of the departments of electronics, and ocean development, hitherto forming a part of the 'S & T Plan' were split into an 'S & T' plan and components of socio-economic plans. Some of the departments, like environment and non-conventional energy sources, were even shifted to the administrative and planning structures of socio-economic ministries.

Changed perception of overlap between different policy regimes also manifests in the allocation of financial resources to science and technology. Government funds for science and technology in India are channelled through two blocks. One block is of 'S & T agencies' i.e. those without the responsibility for setting up production or service systems and a second block of socio-economic ministries. Generally, 52 per cent of government funds for R & D have been given to the S & T agencies and only 48 per cent to the other agencies. This distribution is going to change. Since 1985, financial institutions are also getting involved in R & D funding. For example, funds for technology development are channelled through financial institutions like the Industrial Development Bank of India (IDBI). The trend which started in 1985 is likely to continue. Comparison with countries like Japan, the United States and West Germany indicates that funds for R & D to the tune of 70 per cent may have to be channelled through socio-economic agencies and financial institutions; as in those countries, 70 per cent of national expenditure for R & D would come through those engaged in production and services. The science and technology policy regime in India will thus become changed and with it the decisionmaking process.

The crucial issue would then be the accommodation process within a restructured science and technology constituency. Decisionmakers accustomed to accommodation and adjustments in a narrower S & T policy regime, to picking up signals of their choice from other regimes, will then have to seek legitimation from a much wider constituency. This constituency would consist not only of leading scientists and researchers but also of those leading social, industrial and economic development.

The process of restructuring of science and technology started in the 1980s is to continue at an increasing pace. The tensions that develop in redefining S & T policy regimes and in the emergence of new constituencies for the legitimation of science and technology decisions will have to be tackled through continued political support and will.

Discussion summary

Stuart Blume

In the discussion it was clear that the issues raised in the chapters in Part I are by no means only academic niceties but are of eminent practical importance. Given the soaring costs of research and development in many fields which are beginning to outstrip the resources of even wealthy countries, the need to choose — to establish priorities — cannot be doubted. But how are these priorities to be established, also in the light of national goals? Should the processes of priority setting differ as between, say, industrial technology, health, and the defence area? No simple answers to these complex issues were given, but on one point there was general agreement. Assessments of the state of the science and technology frontier, however sophisticated methodologically, do not yield priorities for research. At best, they indicate where areas of possible opportunity may lie. This indication might properly be one (important) input into the formulation of national priorities, but not the determining factor.

Regarding the significance of national goals — referred to as 'the philosophical expression of the aspirations of the people' — a number of positions were represented in the discussion. For some participants the notion of attempting logically to derive research priorities from national goals was fruitless and unrealistic. Even though that might be common practice in development planning, it was a notion which inadequately reflected the nature of the research process. To some extent at least (basic) research must remain curiosity driven. Other participants took their cue from the hard realities which confront a country such as India. Resources for R & D are limited, both as a percentage of GNP and absolutely; technology has to be imported and the knowledge needed for effective absorption of imported technologies is crucial; the technological gap between India and the developed world has widened. Perhaps with the approach of the unified European market in 1992 The Netherlands will be faced with similarly harsh choices.

It became clear from the examples which participants introduced into the discussion that *in practice* national goals may be significant for research priorities in a number of different senses. In general, they will have a broad signalling effect, suggesting general areas that from a social point of view merit the attention of the scientific community. In other words, the political discourse partly structures the way in which scientists perceive the world in which they live and their sense of what is important. For this to work requires, of course, that the scientific community be receptive to signals of this sort, motivated to look to interpret its own concerns in terms of the needs of society. If, for one reason or another the scientific community becomes isolated or alienated from society this will thus impede its receptivity to such social signals. Beyond this, however, national goals may on occasion have a more directive effect on scientific work. For example, in the 1960s Indian industrial policy forbade the import of technology. This had clear implications for the CSIR (Council of Scientific and Industrial Research) which developed its R & D policy within the framework of import substitution. That national goals sometimes have a clearly directive significance is also apparent if one thinks about it at a more disaggregated level, sector by sector. Particularly in those sectors in which government has a direct responsibility for policy execution, or for the provision of relevant services, it is likely that R & D will be far more sensitive to changing policy goals. An example given was the area of defence against sea flooding in The Netherlands. Others can be found in the areas relating to defence (where much R & D is typically done 'in house' in government research facilities), to space and (in some countries) to nuclear energy and telecommunications.

The nature of the responsiveness of the science and technology system to national policy goals led logically to a discussion of questions relating to implementation of priorities. It was clear that priorities could be of very different kinds, and the requirements of effective implementation could vary drastically. Provision of money alone would rarely be sufficient, and it was essential to think through the design of an effective strategy. In some cases, for example, it might be a question of developing expertise in an area (such as biotechnology or materials science) as a national resource. This implies that research planning be adequately integrated with educational planning. The expansion of higher educational provision, or the introduction of advanced (masters or doctoral) courses might be of vital importance if manpower adequate to industrial needs is to be produced. Such integration is rarely adequate because of the diverse bodies involved in the two areas of priority setting. Effective implementation might also have very important organizational implications. On occasion, depending on the area of science and technology in question, it might be that the priority can be effectively implemented by simply giving an order, and resources, to an appropriate government research establishment. It might be that what is required lies within the expertise of an establishment which by its very constitution is necessarily responsive to the changing priorities of its political masters. Frequently, however, what is required is not so simply realized. It may be that the appropriate expertise is not located in one single place, or that the relevant scientists are not so readily influenced in their interests. Experience shows that it is important to attend to the organizational features of the science and technology system. Priorities might have little effect because insufficient attention was paid to the motivations of scientists and the conditions for effective scientific work.

The reward and motivation system is an example. Scientists in the basic sciences are naturally influenced to a significant extent by the priorities which their field — internationally — seems to follow. There is obviously something to be said for expressing national priorities in such a way that they are as compatible as possible with questions seen by the scientific community as important. It is also important that research of good quality be valued and be seen to be valued above work of mediocre quality. Despite its apparent triteness, this needs to be said. Honouring top scientific performance may imply modifications to career structures and the criteria for promotion which conflicts with traditional forms of organizational behaviour. A second example of the possible need for organizational restructuring as a prelude to effective implementation relates to inter-organizational relations. Collaboration between organizations with complementary expertise (a university and a government establishment, or a university and industry, for example) is frequently essential to effective implementation. These sorts of collaboration are not always easy to bring about (as a decade of discussions over university–industry relations in Europe shows clearly enough). Thus special measures may need to be taken to establish the institutional conditions within which national priorities for research can become something more than words on paper.

It was clear from the discussion that effective mobilization of the scientific community behind the priorities of society requires accommodation on all sides. The scientific community must acknowledge its responsibilities to the society which provides for it. On the part of government there must be effective recognition of the complex and non-instrumental functions of science, which is also a cultural product and has a critical function for which some independence is needed. There must also be recognition of the various possible strategies of implementation, the need to win the commitment of scientists and the organizational reforms which this may entail.

Part II: National policies towards the R & D systems

Once the place of science policy has been ascertained by having established its links to national goals in areas like economic development, welfare, health, education, agriculture and industrialization and by having made a few fundamental choices as discussed in Part I, the next series of issues arises around the actual policies towards the R & D system at the national level. Such policies concern not only the (often primarily) financial support for selected areas or projects, but also the build-up of appropriate intermediary and research institutions and procedures for continuous policy implementation, as well as the development of a spectrum of subtle instruments to translate priorities and choices into concrete actions and incentives.

Some of the issues of Part I recur here at a more concrete and detailed level, but also some new ones arise as the following list of examples shows. Should the priorities for R & D programmes be defined by researchers or by the government, or should other societal groups have an impact on priorities? How do we measure the effectiveness of our inputs into the R & D system? What is the purpose and position of government-financed research laboratories? What means does a national government have to support R & D and who will profit from this support? Should a government directly fund R & D performed in industry and to what extent? What is the relation between the research and the educational system? In which way can a country benefit from the R & D efforts of another country? What is the appropriate government policy towards importing foreign technology and can we learn from other countries in this respect?

The two chapters, by Professor S.K. Shrivastava and Dr K.V. Swaminathan and by Dr H.J. van der Molen and Dr W. Hutter respectively on the national policies towards the R & D system in India and in The Netherlands respectively, do not pretend to answer these questions exhaustively for both countries. In their careful description and analysis of these policies they indicate both their complex structure and subtle details. For further information on both countries' policies the country reports of Part 5 are also useful.

4 National policies towards the R & D system in India

S.K. Shrivastava and K.V. Swaminathan

INTRODUCTION

India's tradition of higher learning and research dates back to 4000 BC. With major contributions in philosophy, literature, astronomy, mathematics, medicine, material science, arts and music India led the world for centuries, and attracted scholars to its universities from distant places. Although much of this glory was lost during the centuries of foreign rule, many scholars continued their efforts. After independence, science and technology became a national pursuit. The nation committed itself to foster science, technology and education on a massive scale.

Higher education and the intelligentsia nurtured by it have a special role in determining the quality of overall environment. Higher education also supplies a wide range of increasingly sophisticated and ever-changing variety of manpower needed in industry, agriculture, administration and services. Recognizing this, the policy statements related to science and technology issued by the government of India from time to time always emphasized the need for nurturing research in the universities and academic institutions.

POLICY STATEMENTS

The Scientific Policy Resolution adopted on 4 March, 1983[1] clearly states that the aim of the policy will be (i) to foster, promote and sustain by all appropriate means the cultivation of science and scientific research in all its aspects — pure, applied and educational; (ii) to ensure adequate supply within the country of research scientists of highest quality and to recognize their work as an important component of the strength of the nation; (iii) to encourage and initiate, with all possible speed, programmes for the training of scientific and technical personnel on a scale adequate to fulfil the country's needs in science and education, agriculture and industry and defence.

The Technology Policy Statement of the government of India[2] states that Indian science and technology must unlock the creating potential of our people and help in building the India of our dreams. It considers human resources to be our richest endowment and therefore conditions must be created for the fullest expression and utilization of scientific talent. According to the statement, R & D together with science and technology education and training of a high order will be accorded pride of place. The base of science and technology consists of trained and skilled manpower at various levels, covering a wide range of disciplines, and an appropriate institutional, legal and fiscal infrastructure. Consolidation of the existing base and selective strengthening of thrust areas in it is essential. Special attention will be given to the promotion and strengthening of the technology base in newly emerging and frontier areas such as information and material science, electronics, and biotechnology. Education and training to upgrade skills are also of the utmost importance. Basic research and the building of centres of excellence will be encouraged.

The National Policy on Education — 1986[3] recognizes that higher education is a crucial factor for survival as it provides people with an opportunity to reflect on the critical, social, economic, cultural, moral and spiritual issues facing humanity. It contributes to national development by dissemination of specialized knowledge and skills. According to the Policy, research in the universities will be provided enhanced support and steps will be taken to ensure its high quality. Suitable mechanisms will be set up for coordinating research in the universities, particularly in the thrust areas of science and technology, with research undertaken by other agencies. An effort will be made to encourage the setting up of national research facilities within the university system, with proper forms of autonomous management. It further states that research as a means of renovation and renewal of the education process will be undertaken by all higher technical institutions. It will primarily aim at producing quality manpower capable of taking up R & D functions. Research and development will focus on improving present technologies, developing new indigenous ones and enhancing production and productivity.

S & T MANPOWER

During the last four decades, the infrastructure of higher education in the country has grown phenomenally. From a handful of universities and colleges with very limited enrolment capacity at the time of independence, the total number of universities and institutions of national importance has now touched the figure of 179, with a total enrolment of approximately 3.7 million. The annual out-turn of science and technology personnel is approximately 25,000. The number of doctorates awarded per year in science and science-related topics, however, is less than 4,000 and in engineering and technology the number is much smaller (fewer than 500 per year).

Quantitatively, in today's world, India has a large science and technology manpower. A wide-based infrastructure for science and technology has also been built. However, when viewed in the context of the pace of development worldwide and the dimensions of the problems of national development confronting us, it is apparent that the gap between India and advanced countries has widened. India's rank in the list of industrialized nations is also dropping. Perhaps one of the most important causes for this widening gap is lack of adequate resources and infrastructure for research in the universities/institutions. Although the nation now spends about 1 per cent of its GNP (against 2–3 per cent in advanced nations), on R & D, only 5–6 per cent of this amount (as against 20–30 per cent in advanced nations) is available to higher-education institutes. In absolute terms the R & D budget in Indian universities amounts to about Rs.1 billion/year as against about Rs.200 billion/year spent in the universities in the United States. Even this is restricted to only a few institutions which have the basic infrastructure to undertake projects of relevance to science and technology agencies and industry. Universities/institutions lacking proper infrastructure for training and research are also unable to attract and retain talented faculty. Many able people who could become leaders in research are lost to other professions or go abroad.

One of the important factors in the development of a country is the number of persons in the R & D profession. It is estimated that in the United States there are sixty-seven R & D professionals for every 10,000 persons. The corresponding figure for Japan is sixty-three; for West Germany fifty; France, forty; the United Kingdom, thirty-two. In India it is fewer than three R & D professionals per 10,000 persons. A clear, coordinated effort is needed for development of R & D manpower in order to match in number and quality of training the needs of the country. It may be emphasized that R & D culture is best introduced in the formative stage of education and not at a later stage when rigid orientation has already occurred. There is a need for a determined effort to attract some of the best students to take up research as a career.

It is also noted that there is not adequate cooperation and collaboration between universities, research laboratories and industry. It is noted that within the country there are enormous gaps in the infrastructural facilities and capabilities between what is obtained in specialized scientific agencies and national laboratories, in the industrial undertakings and in the educational system. The major science and technology agencies and R & D units of both public and private industries draw heavily on the academic sector for their manpower needs. Yet, with some exceptions like the ministry of science and technology they do not do enough financially or otherwise to support R & D manpower development and/or research in the academic sector. Poor libraries, an inadequate information system, ill-equipped laboratories, absence of computational facilities are endemic to the majority of educational institutions. This situation needs to be remedied rapidly if those emerging from the Indian educational system are to be effective in the national research and production systems. Studies have been initiated to analyse the phenomenon of 'brain-drain' from some of the premier Indian educational institutions.[4]

MAJOR SCIENTIFIC AGENCIES AND DEPARTMENTS

The ministry of science and technology is the primary ministry dealing with science and technology. It has three departments under it: the department of science and technology, the department of scientific and industrial research and the department of biotechnology. Other departments dealing with scientific and technological aspects include the departments of atomic energy, electronics, space, environment, non-conventional energy sources, ocean development and the ministry of human resources development. In addition there are several other ministries such as health, industry and communication which have components of S & T in their activities.

The responsibilities entrusted to the department of science and technology include formulation of policy guidelines in science and technology, promotion of new areas of S & T, international scientific and technological affairs, S & T entrepreneurship development. In addition the department also undertakes the funding of scientific and technological surveys. The department of biotechnology is the apex body identified to coordinate and oversee development of biotechnology and to prepare and implement a coordinated programme in multidisciplinary areas of biotechnology. The department of scientific and industrial research has one of the major scientific agencies dealing with scientific and industrial research, the Council of Scientific and Industrial Research (CSIR). It also undertakes a wide range of activities related to technology promotion, development and utilization. The CSIR has a network of about forty national laboratories and more than one hundred field centres. The CSIR group of laboratories is engaged in major areas of research: physical and earth science, chemical science, biological science, engineering science and information science. It is engaged in several facets of the technology missions as well as the pursuit of national programmes.

The department of atomic energy is responsible for R & D in the field of atomic energy and has under it major centres such as the Bhabha Atomic Research Centre (BARC), the Indira Gandhi Centre for Atomic Research and the Centre for Advanced Technology. BARC, the largest single scientific establishment, provides R & D backing for nuclear power programmes and undertakes a wide range of R & D activities in scientific disciplines including development and application of radio isotopes and isotope techniques in medicine and industry and many other areas. Space research programmes are implemented through the department of space and these include satellite communications, satellite remote sensing and development and operation of indigenous satellites. The department also undertakes development of launch vehicles for a wide variety of satellites. The department of electronics is the executive wing of the electronic commission which deals with formulation of policies and programmes for the development of electronics and also directs the implementation of such programmes. The department of environment serves as a focal point in the administrative structure of the government for planning, promotion and coordination of environment programmes. The department of ocean development is entrusted with the responsibilities of promotion of R & D in the marine sector, map resources of economic zones, deep seabed mining and Antarctic research. The department of non-conventional energy sources has promoted research, development and utilization of solar energy and has also set up a large number of biogas plants in the country.

The Indian Council of Agricultural Research (ICAR) is the apex agency for all agricultural and animal husbandry research and education in the country and has thirty-six central institutes. The ICAR provides linkages with the ministry of agriculture. The Indian Council of Medical Research is the apex body for formulating, coordinating and promoting biomedical research. Its research is intra-mural and extra-mural. The council has eighteen research institutes and centres addressing themselves to specific health topics. The Defence Research and Development Organization has a network of over forty laboratories and other technical cells and covers a wide range of disciplines such as aeronautics, rockets, missiles, electronics and instrumentation, armament technology, computer science, material science, food and agriculture.

There are research laboratories attached to specific ministries such as the Research Design and Standards Organization (RDSO) to the ministry of railways, the Telecommunication Research Centre to the ministry of communication, the Indian Statistical Institute to the ministry of planning, etc. There are over one hundred such institutions dealing with specific subject areas. The major part of R & D funds are utilized by the major scientific research organizations such as the Council of Scientific and Industrial Research, the Indian Council of Agricultural Research, the Indian Council of Medical Research, the Defence Research Development Organization, the Space Research Organization and Atomic Energy.[5] (For details see the Country Report on India in Part V of this book.)

MEASURES TO SUPPORT SCIENTIFIC RESEARCH

Recognizing research as an essential component of higher education, several initiatives have been taken by the University Grants Commission, the department of education and the ministry of science and technology to promote research in academic institutions. These initiatives include:

- Increased allocation for research
- Direct central assistance to universities/institutions
- Enhancement of research fellowships/associateships
- Modernization of laboratories
- Support for research in thrust areas
- Creation of advanced centres for research in universities/institutions
- Creation of major research facilities with cooperative and autonomous management
- Interlinking of libraries, computers and information systems into a nation-wide abstracting service
- Promotion of international cooperation and collaboration in research
- Cultural exchange programmes
- Support of faculty members for participation in national and international conferences
- Support for the organization of conferences
- Support for publication of research work.

However, the total resources made available still remain much smaller than the actual requirement. Efforts are being made to find additional resources from other science and technology departments and industry. The need for much greater interaction between academic institutions, national laboratories and industry is being emphasized at the highest level. Some of the possibilities under examination include (i) setting up of laboratories and advanced centres by industry and research agencies on the campuses of higher educational institutions; (ii) sophisticated and expensive research facilities to be treated as national facilities and made accessible to universities; (iii) creation of a data base and coordination of all efforts; (iv) better technology forecasting and assessment of research; (v) re-orientation of research efforts to meet the basic needs of the country and its advancement and (vi) encouragement towards international cooperation in research and development.

With a view to promoting the growth of research and development activities in industry and non-profit orientated organizations, various measures have been developed. Some of the provisions in the Income Tax Act have been designed to encourage research and development.

Under the Indian Income Tax Act, scientific research associations and institutions which undertake scientific research can collect donations, which are exempt from taxation by the donor, subject to the organization being approved by the secretary in the ministry of science and technology. Since 1974, the department of science and technology (now the department of scientific and industrial research) under the ministry of science and technology has been dealing with such approval of institutions engaged in natural and other applied sciences. The authority for approving institutions in medicine, agriculture and the social sciences was given to the Indian Council of Medical Research, the Indian Council of Agricultural Research and the Indian Council of Social Sciences Research respectively. The implementation of the scheme was reviewed by the government in 1981–2. Since the administration of the scheme through different prescribed authority gave rise to problems of non-uniformity and inconsistent interpretations, the government decided to transfer the work relating to approval of institutions in medicine, agriculture, and social sciences to the department of science and technology. Accordingly, the DST became a single prescribed authority in June 1982. With the formation of the department of scientific and industrial research in the ministry of science and technology in 1985, this responsibility is now vested with the department of scientific and industrial research (DSIR).

With DSIR becoming the single prescribed authority, the advantage of the scheme came to light. It was noted, among other factors, that the scheme had enabled the establishment of institutes like the Indian Institute of Sciences, Bangalore; the Tata Institute of Fundamental Research, Bombay; the Shri Ram Institute of Scientific Research, New Delhi; the Bombay Natural History Society, Bombay; the United Planters Association of South India, Coonoor; the Bombay Textile Research Association, Bombay; the Tuberculosis Society of India, New Delhi and so on. Some of these institutions are well known internationally. Mention may also be made of the Indian Institute of Science, Bangalore which was set up by Tatas and benefited through donations under the Income Tax Act. Its reputation hardly needs any elaboration. A similar case is the Tata Institute of Fundamental Research, Bombay which originated from private benevolence and later was taken over by the department of atomic energy. The department of scientific and industrial research has on its active list about 500 notified institutions. These institutions employ over 10,000 persons. Their activities, which include product development and product improvement, have saved a considerable amount of foreign exchange. By 1986 they had registered forty-one patents and published about 800 papers. They conducted about 400 seminars and conferences as well as seventy training classes. Apart from the above, these institutions have played a significant role in generating positive scientific attitudes in India.

Foundations approved by the prescribed authority for conducting scientific research cover a wide range of research activities including mathematics, physics, chemistry, botany, crops such as cotton, sugar-cane, oil-seeds, tea, medical topics such as tuberculosis, diabetes, ophthalmology, cancer, cardiology, etc. An account of the research carried out by these institutions in such divergent areas has been brought out by the DSIR.[6] Data covers the facilities available in terms of manpower, equipment, achievements claimed by such foundations, etc. According to the Direct Tax Act, 1987 certain sections have been withdrawn and other sections introduced relating to scientific research associations/institutions. The details and guidelines for approval under the new section of the IT Act are being worked out.

IN-HOUSE R & D IN INDUSTRY

The government has taken several measures to establish workable linkages between the national laboratories system and industry. One such instrument has been the measures taken for promoting industrial research in industry itself. Several incentives have also been provided which encourage and make it financially attractive for private-sector industrial units to establish their own in-house R & D centres.

A scheme for granting recognition to the in-house R & D units in the industrial sector and private- or public-funded research and development laboratories was operated by the department of science and technology from 1973. This activity is now being handled by the newly formed department of scientific and industrial research under the ministry of science and technology. The DSIR has so far recognized more than 1,000 in-house R & D units in various sectors such as chemicals, electrical and electronics, mechanical, automotive and textiles.[7] One of the objectives of this scheme is to provide a liberalized import facility to recognised R & D units. Under the Open General Licence these laboratories can now import their requirements such as equipment, components, raw materials, etc. to carry out research work in order to upgrade the technology and effect improvements in the manufacturing process, introduce new production processes, develop substitutes for imported items.

The in-house R & D units are distributed throughout the country. A majority of the in-house R & D units are located in and around major cities. The expenditure incurred by in-house R & D units in industry has steadily increased. During 1980–1 it was estimated to be US$2 billion for over 600 units. By 1985–6 it was of the order of US$5 billion. It is estimated that the present R & D expenditure of the 1,015 recognized R & D units is over US$5.5 billion of which 40 per cent is accounted for by about 100 public-sector R & D units and about 60 per cent by over 900 units in private and joint sectors.[8]

There has been a steady increase in R & D manpower employment in the in-house R & D units. By 1975–6 about 13,000 personnel were employed by nearly 400 units. By 1981–2 the figure was over 41,000 for about 750 units. The present estimated manpower for over 1,000 in-house R & D units is over 45,000.

The in-house R & D centres have created impressive infrastructure facilities including sophisticated instrumentation and equipment facilities as well as pilot plant facilities for carrying out high-level R & D work relating to the manufacturing activities of the firms. It is estimated that the R & D assets possessed by in in-house units is over Rs.600 crores at present. Some of the sophisticated equipment facilities available are: scanning electron microscopes; computerized X-ray diffraction and X-ray fluorescence analysers; ultra-violet, visible, infrared, vacuum emission, nuclear magnetic resonance (NMR) and atomic absorption spectrophotometers; chromatographs; thermoanalytical equipment; creep measuring and high-temperature evaluation equipment; microprocessor developed systems; electronic and electrical testing and evaluation equipment; custom-built test rigs; colour matching computers; mechanical and fatigue testing equipment; programme-controlled high-temperature furnaces, etc. Most of the R & D units also have good library facilities of their own and subscribe to a number of periodicals and journals.

A large number of in-house R & D centres have initiated new process developments, product development, material and energy conservation, fuel economy, import substitution, export promotion, foreign exchange savings and training and generation of manpower within the industry. The DSIR have begun to assess the contributions towards national development made by the in-house R & D centres.

As part of the scheme of granting recognition to in-house R & D units in the industrial sector, the DSIR has now instituted 'National Awards' for R & D efforts in industry. The establishment of these awards will give due recognition to such contributions and further impetus to the R & D tempo in industry. The following annual awards were instituted in 1987 by the department of scientific and industrial research:

(a) Four awards for in-house R & D units for their outstanding achievements in the field of industrial research, one each for (i) chemical and allied sectors; (ii) the electrical and electronic sector (iii) the mechanical and automotive sector and (iv) the metallurgical and other process industries' sector.
(b) One award for the best effort made by the industry for successful commercialization of public-funded R & D.

The second award is open to all sectors. These awards will be in the form of medals and shields along with citations given to industrial R & D units for a particular year. In assessing the performance, notable achievements related to selected successfully completed projects/

technologies commercialized by the applicant firm will be taken into account.

R & D TO ABSORB IMPORTED TECHNOLOGY

The Technology Policy Statement set out the principles for acquisition of technology. These are:

(a) Import of technology, and foreign investment in this regard, will continue to be permitted only on a selective basis where need has been established; technology does not exist within the country; the time taken to generate the technology indigenously would delay the achievement of development targets.

(b) The government may, from time to time, identify and notify such areas of high national priority, in respect of which procedures would be simplified further to ensure timely acquisition of the required technology.

(c) There shall be a firm commitment for absorption; adaptation and subsequent development of imported know-how through adequate investment in research and development to which importers of technology will be expected to contribute.

The development of scientific and industrial research (DSIR) has initiated a 'Technology Absorption and Adaptation Scheme' (TAAS) which primarily aims at helping an industry to absorb imported technology and improve the level of technology in use in the country. The scheme is designed to enable an industry to become aware of the existing status of technology, to facilitate technology absorption exercises and to promote and support programmes for absorption, adaptation and up-gradation of imported technologies.

The government has taken various measures for effective absorption of imported technology. A condition in collaboration approvals requires companies to establish design and research facilities to avoid continued dependence on foreign technology. Where technology payments are over Rs.20 million it is obligatory for firms to involve R & D personnel in technology acquisition; and they should submit a programme for technology absorption, adaptation and improvement; set up in-house R & D facilities recognized by the DSIR or enter into a long-term consultancy management with a relevant R & D institution in the country.

The main thrust of the TAAS is to support and promote measures towards absorption of imported technologies, and adaptation of products and processes relevant to domestic requirements as well as for exports. It will assist units in identifying at early stages of the collaboration the crucial ingredients of imported technology and the potential areas for further product and process innovation. The major objectives of the TAAS are: (i) to reduce the necessity for further import of technology after having it in use over a long period; (ii) to upgrade imported technology, incorporating improvements identified during its use; (iii) to promote the diffusion and export of imported technologies which have been assimilated or adapted; (iv) to strengthen the base for selecting and negotiating appropriate and competitive technology where import of technology is considered desirable; and (v) to study and evaluate efforts in implementation of technology absorption and adaptation programmes related to imported technology.

The scheme is intended to strengthen the R & D base of the industry through partial assistance/support so as effectively to absorb and assimilate the imported technology. The TAAS has a major role to play in the attainment of technological self reliance in the area of imported technology. Its main function is to provide catalytic support for accelerated absorption and adaptation of imported technologies by the industrial units. The technological capabilities built up through the support under TAAS will enable the development of better national negotiating capacity for the import of technology on more favourable terms and conditions than otherwise, especially in the case of closely held technologies.

MEASURES FOR ENCOURAGING INDIGENOUS TECHNOLOGY

The Technology Policy Statement had identified a variety of issues which in turn required to be translated to specific actions. In order to examine these concepts the government has established a Technology Policy Implementation Committee (TPIC) whose composition includes secretaries of important economic ministries, in addition to those in science and technology. The TPIC has dealt with a very large number of important issues which include: establishment of an R & D research and development fund; need to promote international R & D collaboration; utility of a technology forecasting system; the mode of establishment of a system for technology assessment; the utility of a technology data bank; the need for protection of industrial property; waste utilization; evolving concepts relating to development contracts; suggestions and guidelines in technology absorption; and mechanisms in ensuring an efficient technology delivery system.

The government of India has taken clear steps to promote and support indigenous technology. These include introduction of several schemes and mechanisms. A scheme to encourage the establishment of in-house research and development units in industry has already been dealt with. This scheme enables industry to establish a good interface with the academic and research institutions on the one hand and production units on the other hand. Another measure provides support to establish scientific institutions; contributions made to such institutions are exempt from taxes. The government has also provided incentives for utilization of technology developed within the country; this was provided as an investment allowance on the cost of plant and machinery installed in an enterprise using indigenous developed technology. There are provisions by which public undertakings can provide equity in establishing new units using indigenous technology. Another provision relates to development projects in which an invention made at laboratory level can be experimented on at full scale with government participation. Price control mechanisms give due recognition to indigenous research efforts. Indigenously developed technology will also be free from normal problems relating to licensing. There are a variety of other facilities provided by the government system to encourage indigenous efforts. Currently a substantial part of the R & D efforts are funded directly by the government. By virtue of the new incentives provided, the industrial units in the country have started R & D projects and currently 20 per cent of the national expenditure on R & D is contributed by industry.

The ministry of science and technology has evolved several schemes in the area of technology utilization. Mention has already been made of the promotional measures to facilitate the establishment of in-house R & D centres. A new scheme mentioned above called technology absorption and adaptation (TAAS) has been evolved to absorb imported technology. A scheme on the national register of foreign collaboration has also been initiated which provides information on past records of joint ventures and the means for making reports on technologies in several industries with a view to assisting in further acquisition of technology. A scheme on transfer and trading in technology has been evolved with a view to increasing technical cooperation with many developed countries and in this, efforts are made to assemble technology profiles of different countries and to facilitate the mutual exchange of experience and technology. There is a scheme on promotion and support to consultancy services to recognize the important role of consultancy organizations in technology transfer.

The technology policy statement had said that a strong central group would be constituted to undertake technology forecast and technology assessment studies. Where big investments are involved or a large volume of production is envisaged it will be incumbent on the ministry or agency concerned to provide a technology forecast covering its requirements over a ten-year or longer period and to evolve a strategy for development based on priorities. Following this the government established the Technology Information Forecasting and Assessment Council (TIFAC) in November 1986. The main objectives of TIFAC are to encourage various technology forecasting and technology assessment activities in the country and to ensure their follow up in terms of suggesting strategies for technological development and to draw up programmes of practical R & D and the adaptation of technologies.

In technology development, linkages are often very important considerations. In the context of the system in India these linkages could be identified as the four corners of a square. One corner is the important role of research activities. Currently these include the research laboratories established under the various organizations like the Council of Scientific and Industrial Research, the Indian Council of Medical Research, the Indian Council of Agricultural Research, institutes of higher learning like the Indian Institute of Technology and over 1,000 in-house R & D centres. On the second corner one could identify several agencies dealing with technology development. Mention may be made of public undertakings like the National Research Development Corporation, which is one of the largest technology sellers of indigenous technology, the National Small Industries Corporation, the National

Industrial Development Corporation and many other public-sector enterprises. On the third corner one could identify a large number of financial institutions like the Industrial Development Bank of India, the Industrial Finance Corporation of India, the Industrial Credit and Investment Corporation of India and a large number of nationalized banks. The fourth corner deals with the scope and support to consultancy development organizations. These include the Association of Consulting Engineers, which is a body of professional individual consultants; the National Association of Consulting Engineers who are a group of consultancy firms who may also undertake contracting; the Federation of Indian Export Organizations whose consultancy wing looks after the export of products and services. With the cooperation and association of all the three agencies mentioned a new Consultancy Development Centre has also been established with the support of the ministry of science and technology.

POLICY SUPPORT

The Scientific Policy Resolution of 1958 and the more recent Technology Policy Statement of 1983 are important landmarks in the government announcing its policy support in the area of S & T. In India we do not have an act in the area of S & T or even the area of technology transfer. Therefore, a substantial part of the government's intentions regarding S & T rely on the Scientific Policy Resolution and the Technology Policy Statement. Since these do not have any regulatory powers, wherever regulation is required recourse has to be made to other acts and laws of the country. These are substantially found in the Import and Export Regulation Act, the Industrial Development and Regulation Act, the Income Tax Act, the Foreign Exchange Regulation Act, the Monopolies and Restrictive Practices Act, the Patent Act, the Trade and Merchandise Marks Act, the Environmental Act, the Water Pollution Act, the R & D Levy Act etc.

Currently fiscal incentives are available in the area of scientific research and to support scientific research associations and their incentives. For example, the Income Tax Act provides for tax incentives for industrial units engaged in scientific research. Customs duty exemption is available for scientific research institutions when acquiring their assets. Enhanced investment allowance/depreciation is admissible on the cost of plant and machinery installed in manufacturing units using indigenously developed technology. These are being reviewed continuously.

It is widely recognized that a limited protection from unfair competition is essential for nascent industrial units. This could include protection from well-established units, trading companies marketing foreign products under established brand names or foreign companies dumping products in India for brief periods. Such protection from unfair competition may involve banning certain imports for limited periods. Further, many manufacturing units cannot hope to make all components under one roof. Some of them necessarily will require the importation of a limited set of components. It has repeatedly been pleaded that the customs duty structure must be such that it should encourage maximizing efforts to add value within the country. Thus customs duty on raw materials should be lower than that on components, which again will be much lower than on finished products. The difference between the groups must be sufficiently marked to promote indigenization of components and materials successively.

In many countries the government is one of the largest buyers. This is so in India. Preferential treatment in government purchases for technologies based on indigenous technology or any purchase of demonstration units made by indigenous efforts needs to be increased to promote a demand for indigenous technology.

New technology development necessarily will have to go through the process of trial and correction. At this stage the feedback from the market after use for some time is necessary. In such circumstances, development contracts are provided by the government and user departments to promote the development of new products and their introduction to the market. Large purchases should be made by granting development contracts, and upgrading their specifications which will not only promote a minimum size critical for promoting development work but will also enable successive upgradation and quality to the consumer. However, this mechanism has not been used in a significant manner in the present system.

Support for innovative activity involves risk taking since only a few of the innovations would finally turn out to be successful ventures. The past experience in many other countries also seem to indicate small groups are more effective in their innovative process. Support to such small groups also requires a change in lending concepts or the extension of grants. Some of the recent initiatives of the banks have opened up opportunities for directing support to innovations. This must be pursued and should be more broadly based to reach small innovative groups.

CONCLUSION

Science and technology initiatives have received continued support from the government, particularly during the last three or four decades.

The prime minister is also the minister of science and technology which gives a clear indication of the commitment to science and technology. The prime minister has a scientific adviser who is a member of the Planning Commission. He also has a Science Advisory Council composed of a few members both from the industry and the scientific institutions of excellence. The ministry of science and technology has three departments and, in addition, there are a few other departments which are under the prime minister: electronics, space, ocean development and atomic energy. Components of S & T are present in several other ministries and departments such as agriculture, health, industry, housing and human resources development.

From time to time, several policy statements have been issued which have a direct bearing on the R & D system in the country and in particular the industrial policy of 1956, the SPR of 1958 and the TPS of 1983. While India has no statute or act for S & T, or for technology transfer, the necessary provisions relating to these can be found in several other acts. The policies of the government towards the R & D system have concentrated on building a sound S & T infrastructure which could lead to technological self-reliance.

REFERENCES

1. Scientific Policy Resolution, March 1958, Government of India, New Delhi, India.
2. Technology Policy Statement, January, 1983, Department of Science and Technology, Ministry of Science and Technology, Government of India, New Delhi.
3. The National Policy on Education, 1986, Ministry of Human Resources Development, Government of India, New Delhi.
4. Pilot Study on Magnitude and Nature of the Brain Drain of Graduates of the Indian Institute of Technology, Bombay, Department of Science and Technology, Government of India, New Delhi (1988).
5. Research and Development Statistics, 1986–7, Department of Science and Technology, Government of India, New Delhi.
6. A Profile of Scientific Research Institutions, March 1987, Department of Scientific and Industrial Research, Ministry of Science and Technology, New Delhi.
7. Directory of in-house R & D in industry, December 1987, department of scientific and industrial research, ministry of science and technology, New Delhi.
8. 'In-house R & D in Industry', *Annual Report, 1987–8*, Ch. 4, department of scientific and industrial research, ministry of science and technology, New Delhi.

5 National policies towards the R & D system in The Netherlands

H.J. van der Molen and *W. Hutter*

INTRODUCTION

For the last 300 to 400 years science and technology in The Netherlands have been publicly discussed, reflecting the requirements of society for suitable technologies to support national activities, for example an interest in geography and astronomy arose as early as the fifteenth and sixteenth centuries as a result of the activities of the Dutch merchant and naval fleets; civil engineering developed to support the battle against the sea; the interest in agriculture reflected the highly developed agrarian sector.

For the economic development of The Netherlands following the Second World War, priority was given to the creation and maintenance of human resources. In this way scientific and technological manpower could be secured for agriculture and industry based on the newest scientific and technological developments. In addition to supporting the requirements of society and industry The Netherlands have always been a meeting place (and frequently a shelter) for the different cultural and scientific schools in Europe. This has instilled a tradition of great interest in basic research which has made it possible for a small country like The Netherlands (contributing only 1–2 per cent of scientific activities worldwide) to be reasonably informed, through active participation, in most scientifically important areas.

There are many aspects of national policies towards the R & D system in The Netherlands which would justify a comparison with national policies in other countries. The present chapter aims to present some (necessarily brief and incomplete) information and thoughts about the situation in The Netherlands as background for further discussions on:

- the role of the government
- the relationship between higher education and research
- priorities
- enhancement of quality
- diffusion of scientific information

ROLE OF THE GOVERNMENT

At present the minister for education and science is responsible for the coordination of science policy. This coordination is carried out following a basic model in which every minister is responsible for his policy, and related policy proposals from different departments are correlated to the main points by the coordinating minister. Thus the minister for economic affairs is responsible for technology policy and also for inter-ministerial coordination in this field. He is particularly charged with industrially orientated research and with energy research. The preparations for political decisionmaking at ministerial level on science and technology policy are structured, as in many other countries, through a committee at cabinet level which is responsible for the general coordination between the various government ministers and has to ensure policy coordination. In The Netherlands this ministerial committee is chaired by the prime minister.

Government-supported organizations and institutions of research and education which concentrate mainly on basic and strategic research include thirteen universities including three universities of technology, one agricultural university and one open university; eight 'teaching' hospitals; The Netherlands Organization for Scientific Research (NWO) and the Royal Netherlands Academy of Arts and Sciences (KNAW).

In addition to the universities there is a relatively extensive system of non-university research institutes. In the so-called 'para-university institutes' the emphasis is mainly on basic strategic research. In other research institutes the emphasis lies primarily on applied strategic research, particularly in the physical, agricultural and technical sciences. However, applied research, often on commission, in the social and medical sciences fields takes place extensively in the universities as well. Government-supported non-university research is carried out in some 180 institutes, which are characterized by their multifarious nature, a wide range of relationships and modes of financing.

With regard to relationships between the institutes themselves, and between these institutes and the universities, there is in addition to intensive cooperation, a wide-ranging diversification of research activities (for example in the field of environmental research) and even, in some cases, distinct competition.

Government policy for research has as important main objectives:

— promoting quality standards, with the international context as a touchstone;
— reinforcing orientation towards external questions in the medium- and long-term perspective;
— increasing coordination, cooperation and distribution of tasks in the research system;
— promoting efficient and effective operations in research institutes; attaining the best possible financial structure, investment policy, staffing policy and management.

The Dutch government aims in particular at the promotion of processes of change which contribute towards the above objectives including:

(a) the structure of the R & D potential, namely the organization of finance, administration and decisionmaking;
(b) the orientation of research efforts through stimulation policy and promotion of research programming;
(c) the transfer of knowledge to users, for example by promoting the input of scientific and technical information.

RELATIONSHIP BETWEEN HIGHER EDUCATION AND RESEARCH

One of the main instruments for science policy is scientific manpower: there would be no research if there were no research workers carrying out the research in their laboratories or in their research institutes. This means two things: first, the importance of the relation between the educational system, that is the universities and the research system has to be stressed; and second, a good research management in the scientific institutes — thus the need to put the right man in the right place — is very important.

Historically the university system in The Netherlands has been the most important government-supported institutional structure for both the training of scientists and actual research. Until the 1970s active participation of university students in research during their pre-doctoral training was the rule rather than the exception. In certain disciplines, particularly in the natural and life sciences, many graduates would continue working in the universities to obtain a doctoral degree. As a result of an increasing number of students entering universities in the 1970s and the resulting capacity problems, a restructuring of higher education has been realized which will not offer every undergraduate the possibility of participating in research.

At present all university curricula should lead to a first university degree after four years. During this first phase students will hardly participate in research. For a limited number of graduates (in the order of 5 to 10 per cent, but varying for different disciplines) there will be the possibility of continuing for a second four-year phase, including research activities, which should normally result in a doctoral degree. This phase can accommodate approximately 5,000 students which, with a four-year turnover, should theoretically permit 1,250 students per annum to start a research career in this way.

Thus, the Dutch universities find themselves nowadays in an extensive process of reorientation from the traditional continental European university with intricate links or unity between education and research to a more Anglo-American system with post-graduate institutes financed for their research activities, and educating doctoral students.

It was also (and frequently still is) the rule that the academic staff at universities were selected mainly on the basis of their scientific expertise and performance. This made universities the centres for basic research. During the last forty years, however, many independent government-supported research institutions have evolved. This, in addition to the changes within the universities, has made the role of universities in the overall national research effort less dominant, albeit they still play a leading role in many scientific areas. Also, the minister of education and science has an important policy instrument at his disposal for university research in the form of organization of finance for the universities. This policy instrument includes the following aspects:

(i)   the universities are to be able to act as autonomous bodies,
(ii) the research plans for the universities are to take into account national discipline-by-discipline recommendations, and
(iii) a substantial part of the research projects at universities is to be financed by the national research organization (NWO) which, unlike the universities, need not consider teaching aspects.

Consequently, research activities are funded through a system of 'multiple financing': for funding, researchers may apply to different sources with different decisionmaking procedures. The first source of money is allocated directly by the minister of education and science. The universities receive these funds as a part of their total budget. Government funds are still distributed among the universities as a lump sum, but a part of this sum is earmarked for research that has been affirmatively assessed by an external review; these earmarked funds are protected from budgetary cuts by both the universities and the minister of education and science.

The second source of funding is also by government grant, but allocated to the universities through independent organizations such as NWO and STW (Foundation for Technical Science). NWO is the more important: its foundations and study groups play a major role in the national coordination of university research. Basic stipulations in the arrangement are (i) the funding system should be controlled by the scientists themselves and (ii) scientific research should *not* be dissociated from the universities. About half of NWO's total budget is used to finance projects in university research through this second source. A large number of these projects last for three or four years and are undertaken by Ph.D. students. Most projects are based on proposals which have been positively vetted by (expert) review, but sometimes NWO itself takes the initiative to finance a particular project.

The third source of funding comes from a miscellaneous collection of financial bodies: private foundations, government agencies, industry etc. Usually, the object of research projects funded by these sources is to solve specific problems for anyone willing to pay for this service, and are generally referred to as 'contract research' projects. By carrying out contract research, the research capacity of a university can be increased, and the university scientist becomes better informed about problems in society.

The total research capacity of the universities comprises approximately 11,000 full-time equivalents of scientific personnel, of which 7,000, 1,700 and 2,200 are financed by the first, second and third sources, respectively. In the near future, two kinds of document will occupy a central place in university planning: the development plans of the individual universities and the higher education and research plan of the government. In their development schemes the universities write down their plans and intentions taking into account authoritative views relevant to the universities' activities and to previous higher-education plans. The higher education plan, on the other hand, contains the government's medium-term provision for higher education, and is based on developing plans for universities, signals which the government receives from its advisory bodies or visions of its own.

PRIORITIES

Shortage of money for research at all levels inevitably results in discussions about priorities. Such discussions, however, are not the prerogative of private organizations where research is expected to fit the aims of the organization, or of public institutions (including governments) for which the investment of often large sums of public money justifies a discussion about the priorities for the public at large of the research to be done; also the individual scientist has (often tacitly) to set his priorities in any research he considers.

Even if the need for priorities in research is generally accepted, the methods for determining them are many and variable. The Dutch government has recently emphasized the need for individual organizations to consider their activities in the context of nationally agreed priorities in addition to their own priorities resulting from the aims of the organization. The government has supported this policy by specific measures of 'rewards and punishments' to influence the behaviour and orientation of the research community at large.

In the context of science policy, an overall system of priorities is gradually developing. One of the first effects of this can be found in recent science budgets, the annual policy statements of the minister of education and science. These explicitly incorporate recommendations from temporary and permanent intermediary and advisory bodies. Intermediary and advisory bodies contribute to preparation and implementation of research priorities, which lead to the establishment of national programmes. Such organizations offer scope for more indirect forms of influence on research. Intermediary organizations promote the coordination, correlation and programming of research in specific fields.

There should be a continuous process of setting priorities and 'posteriorities' in research, reflecting international developments and the changing needs of society. One way of achieving these goals is the selective promotion by the minister of education and science of specific research items by means of the following sequence of procedures:

(1) In his role as coordinating minister for science policy, the minister initiates an analysis of recent developments in research and actual needs for research; such an analysis may be carried out by the Royal Academy of Arts and Sciences (KNAW), the Advisory Council for science policy (RAWB) or national survey committees. For example, RAWB in 1983 undertook a study concerning the size, productivity and priorities in medical research.

(2) After being advised by KNAW or RAWB, the minister decides which

research items are to be strengthened (or weakened).
(3) Parliament is consulted about his intentions. After this, the minister may react by selective promotion of specific research items.

As part of the national science policy the minister of education and science in his capacity as coordinating minister for science policy has stimulated the development of several so-called 'Spearhead' programmes. These programmes are designed to stimulate research activities in carefully selected fields and have been organized in close collaboration with other government departments, research institutions, social groups and organizations and the private sector. Criteria for selection have included: scientific and/or social interest, innovating character, long-term strategic interest, effect on the structuring of a national research effort. Examples of such Spearhead programmes of science policy are programmes concerned with: health research, soil protection, biotechnology material sciences, earth observation by remote sensing, ageing, labour. These priorities of science policy are of a temporary nature. After four to five years the special support is terminated and it is expected (actually the programmes have this implicit aim) that the continuation of the activities will be integrated in the existing framework.

Apart from these Spearhead programmes several special stimulation programmes have been set up by the minister for economic affairs in the framework of technology policy. Four rather large national technology promoting programmes are carried out in the fields of new materials, biotechnology, medical technology and information technology with the object of promoting applied R & D in private companies. This ministry also promotes cooperative programmes between universities and companies in fields like carbohydrates, metal technology, catalysis, technical ceramics and polymers. Important in these cases is the transfer of knowledge between the university (research) and one or more private companies (application). All these programmes are of a temporary nature, allowing the ministry to promote new technologies successively.

In this way, the distribution of funds among the various research sectors and across the government departments is the outcome of a complicated process of interaction between a wide range of 'actors'. This means that this distribution is the result of a bottom-up process and not of a top-down allocation of funds by the cabinet.

The present system guarantees an active interaction between the different participating organizations in the research system, freely permitting each organization to pursue priorities fitting their own aims and scope of activities as well as to participate in research priorities set by other participants (including government). For example, universities are free to spend a reasonable share of their government support for research on basic sciences of their own choice, but another part of their support has to meet specific quality requirements which are set and evaluated by external experts. If these requirements are not met the university can lose this part of their grant. It is obvious that many universities are also redirecting their own efforts to attract a larger share of the money available for priorities (including the conditionally financed research programmes). The increasing influence of the European Communities also stimulates this development. Similar arrangements apply to the interaction between government and other research organizations, and between research funding organizations such as The Netherlands Organization for Scientific Research (NWO) and the universities. Of course it is important that despite the interaction between the different participating organizations a sufficient degree of freedom is retained for the universities, especially for the fundamental research carried out in these institutions.

ENHANCEMENT OF QUALITY

One of the aims of government policy in The Netherlands towards R & D has been to promote the quality of research. This aim was particularly relevant until about 1975 when government support for research was given mainly as a lump sum (a total of 500–1,000 million guilders annually) with the tacit understanding that universities and other research organizations would use the support for high-quality research. However, neither the aims and/or subjects nor the results (published papers, etc.) of the research were accounted for. Recently increasing emphasis has been placed on visible and generally accepted criteria for quality evaluation — indeed to such an extent that some scientists occasionally complain about the heavy administration burden in applying for and accounting for research support. However, this (often understandable) criticism about the bureaucracy involved in the administration of research plans and results should not detract from the importance of obtaining such administrative data for evaluating research quality.

It has often, but erroneously, been assumed that 'science' or 'scientific performance' is synonymous with 'quality'. History, including very recent events, has given ample evidence that scientists are liable to make errors. Not only 'reputable' errors (inherent in the process of even the most meticulously executed scientific investigation) but also disreputable errors, varying from gross neglect to deliberate fraud. When science was considered as a respectable private hobby for the happy few that were interested and could afford it, the public at large and public institutions were scarcely interested in the performance of scientists and the scientific community. However, at present (in a democratic society) science depends for its support to a large extent on public opinion and public funds and has an enormous effect on society. This development has also created a public interest and responsibility in the quality of scientific performance, which was previously considered the responsibility mainly of the individual scientist or the professional societies.

This development has not yet resulted in a public awareness, or even a generally accepted code among scientists at large, about the most reliable way to evaluate and enhance the quality of scientific performance. However, an increasing number of publications during the past ten to fifteen years, mainly on peer review and so-called bibliometric indicators, have been concerned with different aspects of quality and the evaluation of quality. Also several bodies have attempted to evaluate and compare the quality of different scientific disciplines at the national level.

In The Netherlands, for example, national survey committees have in recent years evaluated the national research activities in such areas as chemistry, biochemistry, biology, physics, health research, economics and law.

In order to evaluate and, if possible, enhance the 'quality' of scientific activities it appears essential that 'quality' is defined in terms of 'technical norms' which guarantee the standard of rationality of the research, testing by empirical evidence (preferably through controlled experiments), reproducibility of results, proper description of methodologies used, proper presentation and interpretation of results, etc. These quality norms should be implicit in all truly scientific procedures and have been discussed in depth by several 'philosophers' of science. It also has to be accepted, however, that there is no 'absolute' or 'natural' standard of quality and that all parameters used will at best reflect a majority or consensus within the scientific discipline involved. The specification of quality in terms of 'technical' norms specifically excludes moral norms or political norms as standards for the quality of behaviour of scientists. The latter 'norms' generally offer no more than rationalizing ideologies which are merely used to justify the self-interests of scientists in comparison to those of other social institutions which also try to justify their activities through their, albeit different moral norms. Such norms may be important, but should not be used in connection with quality. The guarantee for good quality research depends first and foremost on the performance of practising scientists. This will result in an overall enhancement of the quality of research, however, only if the other organizational levels involved in decisions about scientific activities are equally interested in the pursuit of quality.

The following points appear important to stimulate an awareness and application of quality criteria for the evaluation of research.

(1) Criteria for and methods to perform high-quality research should be taught at all levels of student training and should remain a life-long concern of all scientists. It would be naïve, if not pathetic, to discuss the quality of scientific activities if no sense of quality is instilled. Under the ever-increasing pressure of teaching more in less time, it has been all too common to drop from the curricula subjects such as philosophy, methodology and ethics of science. This has caused an undeniable lack of interest (if not lack of understanding) by many scientists in the need for and means to guarantee the quality of their research. Hence a proper (i.e. obligatory) exposure to such subjects is a prerequisite for every potential research student.

(2) If the opportunity to perform research of good quality is lacking, it would be wise to invest in the development of a proper infrastructure and training of scientists rather than perform quality evaluations or to expect that short-term results will result from stimulating research of poor quality.

(3) Working scientists should feel obliged to guarantee the quality of their work by always submitting written research proposals and by publishing their results in well-referred internationally accepted journals. They should ignore those journals that do not offer an acceptable and publicly recognized refereeing system.

(4) Journals, universities and research organizations should base their evaluation of research plans and results on generally accepted and publicly known quality criteria. The results of quality evaluations should be clearly reflected in the 'rewards' or 'punishments' which are given.

(5) Journals, universities and research organizations should compare their quality criteria with those of other comparable institutions in order to know about their rating and the local/national/international level.

(6) Advisory bodies should base their advice also, if not mainly, on the quality of the research involved. They should also (see points 4 and 5) use publicly known criteria and they should inform and stimulate those directly involved in research activities about these criteria. Too often quality requirements are defined only after the research has been performed. This approach has often created unnecessary disappointment about *ex post* expectations that could not be realized because the research had been completed.

(7) At the government level it should be emphasized that research should be of good quality and should be evaluated in a reliable way. Public offices should insist on the use of proper peer review evaluation and the use of proper bibliometric indicators rather than relying on *ad hoc* opinions of individual 'experts'.

Concrete examples of successes or failures in measuring quality of research can be found in the relevant literature.

DIFFUSION OF SCIENTIFIC INFORMATION, TRANSFER OF KNOWLEDGE AND THE EFFECTS OF SCIENCE AND TECHNOLOGY ON SOCIETY

Scientific results which are not communicated will not become part of the scientific process. The diffusion of scientific information is essential for a variety of reasons, including the broadening of the publicly accessible science base, the application of scientific information for technological or social use, or the possibility of evaluating the quality and relevance of results relative to other results (as discussed above.)

The advantages and disadvantages of the many possibilities for communicating scientific results (private communications, congresses, scientific journals, patents, etc.) cannot be discussed in this chapter. Some considerations may be important, however, for the dissemination of scientific information which has been obtained through government-supported research as part of a national policy. At one extreme one will encounter situations where results obtained with public money should be efficiently utilized for public needs, but which usually will not be successful when the results are only published in the international scientific literature. particularly when results are useful for national purposes, special mechanisms for transfer of knowledge to industry or the public at large should be considered. It is an explicit government policy towards the R & D system to enhance the transfer of knowledge from the research institute to possible users. In this respect various mechanisms for transfer have been introduced such as transfer points, spin-off firms, specialized journals or meetings. Also programming committees may play a role in organizing the transfer of knowledge. In this respect specialized journals or meetings aimed at specific national needs may be more effective. In The Netherlands the organization for applied scientific research (TNO) is by law chartered with the responsibility for the transfer of scientific knowledge through several institutes which bring together suppliers and users of scientific information in many industrial and social areas. Also, most universities and other research institutes have installed 'transfer offices' which are active in communicating information obtained within the universities to potential users and vice versa.

At the other extreme one will encounter situations where results, for the very reason that they are important for economic purposes, should probably not be published (or otherwise communicated) before the benefits for the national economy have been secured. The latter consideration has recently stimulated an awareness of the possible need to submit patent applications in advance of publication. Because the individual scientist is not always the best informed or most alert participant in this process, it has been useful to support and coordinate such activities. In addition to the activities of individual universities through their transfer offices, and technological institutes (including TNO), the Foundation for Technical Sciences (STW) in The Netherlands has been very active and successful in pursuing the utilization of scientific information obtained through government-supported research for technological use.

In addition to these activities of research organizations disseminating their results in specific ways, there are some government-supported organizations in The Netherlands which have as their main function the monitoring and dissemination of scientific results for the public at large, for specialized groups in society or for one or more offices in government departments. During the past ten to fifteen years government officials have increasingly called upon research institutions to obtain scientifically based information to formulate their policies ('science for policy').

A rather new and important part of the government policy towards the R & D system may be the establishment of a technology assessment office for assessing the effects on society of present and future technological developments. In The Netherlands such an office — called The Netherlands Organization for Technology Assessment (NOTA) — came into existence one year ago. This independent body initiates opportunities for research into the consequences of science and technology.

SOME CONCLUDING REMARKS

The Dutch system of science and technology policy, comparable to the situation in other countries, demonstrates a process of continuous evolution. This evolution may be characterized by several trends, for example:

(a) There is a shift from a science to a technology policy: government activities become more focused on the application of results of scientific research and on the transfer of knowledge from the research institution to the users. Characteristic of this development is that the ministry of economic affairs has taken over many of the initiatives which were started by the ministry of education and sciences.

(b) International cooperation increases, both officially (for instance in the framework of the European Communities) and informally (scientific networks). The necessity to know at an early stage what is going on in a scientific field in other countries is stressed. Scientists have to go abroad more often, for conferences as well as for temporary exchanges.

(c) Traditionally, Dutch research institutes (and especially the universities) covered a broad spectrum of research interests. Today there is an increasing emphasis on the necessity of making choices: research establishments have to focus upon selected topics and an important criterion in the selection process has to be the possible utilization of the results. A search is going on for 'picking the winners'.

(d) In the universities the traditional link between teaching and research is becoming weaker. The system is developing gradually into the British undergraduate–graduate system; post-graduate research establishments may emerge as a result of this development — more or less a growth into centres of excellence. The universities have been put under strong financial pressure to concentrate their activities and to solicit external private funding through research contracts.

(e) The interference of government in the research system has grown considerably.

Those involved in formulating and executing science and technology policy nowadays face several important problems, for example:

(a) Much scientific equipment is becoming obsolete; important funds are needed to restore an adequate level of instrumentation.

(b) The growth of the system terminated in the seventies; many of the research workers now active are thirty-five to forty years of age and will not leave the institutes in the next fifteen to twenty years. The opportunities for younger scientists have decreased immensely, hence, a problem of a 'lost generation' has emerged.

(c) The research system has to be kept flexible and adaptive. How can we find 'niches' for development of national activities, that is fields of research we are already good in and with good opportunities in the world market?

(d) How can we, in addition to the present 'technological wave', secure an adequate level of funding for the humanities and social sciences?

(e) For a country such as The Netherlands the amount of money spent on R & D seems to be in line with the amounts spent in other industrialized countries. How can we ensure that the transfer of knowledge from the R & D system to possible users is effective and efficient?

Discussion summary

K.V. *Swaminathan*

In the discussion a selected set of the issues dealt with in the papers was taken up. Several of them appeared to have common features in India and The Netherlands. In fact there is a pronounced parallelism as one looks at examples and experience in the two countries and a comparative analysis would therefore be useful. However, there was also a clear recognition that, while these examples are useful, their transferability is valid only up to a certain point, beyond which a specific solution will have to be found for a specific case in question. Transfer of a solution as such from one situation to another is not really possible. The greatest value of a comparison may therefore be the contribution to a deeper understanding of the underlying structure of the issue and therefore of the essential features of a solution. Without an attempt at indicating such an underlying structure the following elements from the discussion can be highlighted.

The problems of society will naturally influence a country's policies and will to a certain extent determine the R & D priorities. The import of technology and the restrictive approach followed thereon in India is a consequence of the appreciation of the specific problems of the country. The role of scientists and the position accorded to them in the Scientific Policy Resolution was reiterated and was illustrated in the present context of several departments of the government being headed by scientists. The need to deal with manpower issues has been highlighted; good education could lead to good science (and vice versa). At the same time there has to be a balance between the freedom given to scientists and accountability; mobility of scientists is necessary to catalyse certain research programmes (diffusion of knowledge). The role of R & D managers is important; it should have a certain relationship to the role to be performed by the research scientists.

As for the lack of adequate manpower, both The Netherlands and India have looked to science and technology as an engine of growth. Both countries have identified gaps in their S & T manpower, and encouraged the more competent students to pursue science. The need was stressed in the discussion to establish cooperation between R & D groups and industry and to create incentives to promote this nexus (even in the form of mobility); this applied equally to the scientists in universities and to those in industry.

With regard to the problems related to diffusion of knowledge, the need was recognized for enlarging the diffusion of scientific information. The present system should be reviewed, the deficiencies in them identified and corrective measures taken. The Indian experience of NISSAT, NRFC and TIFAC were explained. The spin-offs and transfer of knowledge also need to be institutionalized and the role of existing institutions to be reviewed as well as their potential function in relation to other institutions identified, particularly with regard to certain newly emerging institutional arrangements in the financing systems for technology.

The import of foreign technology may imply certain problems and was especially discussed in the Indian context. There is a need for R & D in the industry to improve the level of technology so that it may retain its competitive edge domestically and internationally. This should come from within industry and not be based on subsidies or mandates. The problems become much sharper, however, when access to imported technology is readily available. Here the experience of other developing countries may also be useful. A special problem in the Indian context was recognized relating to ending up with companies with outdated technologies.

The role of state-funded R & D systems was further discussed particularly in the context of their competitiveness and the desire of an enterprise to possess sole ownership of any innovation for marketing purposes. While the historic experience justified the role of state-funded R & D systems, in several countries their effectiveness has become a matter of serious concern. To be effective state-funded R & D must take R & D to the level of commercialization and not leave the effort at bench-level inventions. The role of large companies in R & D funding is an important dimension. The level of expenditure on R & D required in a country and the part of that which should be funded by the state are parameters on which no scientifically based decisions can be made at this stage.

In The Netherlands the TNO (Netherlands Organization for Applied Scientific Research) has been restructured; its present functioning is such that the Dutch government does not monitor research programmes. It broadly sets the guidelines and makes definite allocations for research fields. There is very little government interference and its source of income for the government is only conditional on its having to pursue certain long-term guidelines ('strategic plans') in a five- to ten-year scenario. It appeared that it is absolutely necessary to review the efficacy of the instruments of the science policy periodically and make changes on the basis of experience and perceived needs.

Part III: Practical use of the results of the R & D system

No doubt most people concerned consider that the impact of R & D on society will become still larger, both in developing and in developed countries. But, while some have doubts about this 'scientization' of society, and while some pure scientists may dislike societal questions about the potential application of their work, many are concerned about the repeatedly occurring breaks in the chain between R & D and its practical use. Such breaks appear to occur especially for R & D in government-supported institutes and laboratories, but it has to be admitted that too little is known at all systematically about this phenomenon — even within industries. Is it a real problem? If so, where especially does it occur? Is it to be understood as a lack of practical direction in research, or as a lack of transformation mechanisms in the chain from pure to used research, or, rather the opposite, as a lack of translation of the users' problems into research, or a failing antenna system with the users for the opportunities offered by R & D results? Is it a difference in perceptions, interests, values or incentives between the worlds of research and that of practical users? Is it a lack of communication between them? What is known about strategies and policies to overcome these breaks, which measures have been successful and which efforts can be recommended?

In the chapter by Dr A.D. Wolff-Albers, on the basis of her involvement in science policy at the head of Dutch administration, several ways are mentioned and discussed whereby the government can enhance the practical use of research results from, again, priority setting to institutional arrangements and improved management. Dr Sukh Dev critically analyses the Indian experience, indicating that in agriculture, atomic energy and space technology India has been successful in using its extensive indigenous R & D base, but not in several other areas. Important positive factors for improvement are to be found in scientific infrastructure, project identification, strategy and outlay, motivation, and government policy (tariffs, patents, international cooperation). Dr F. Prakke was asked to work out his comments in the form of a special written contribution in which he draws attention, via applied research to basic research instead of the other way round. Also he distinguishes research-orientated, design-orientated and application-orientated research.

6 The role of government

A.D. Wolff-Albers

INTRODUCTION

Enhancing the practical use of research can refer to several dimensions of science policy, such as the setting of priorities for research, the balance and linkage between fundamental and applied research, the balance between investment in facilities for research and investment in the education of scientists and professionals. There is an executive responsibility of government or performing organizations for transmission of knowledge from universities and public laboratories to users in the public and private sector, but more is needed to restore the synthesis of theory and practice that made for the best contributions by science and engineering to society. Scientists and technologists must be involved in issues on the societal agenda and in defining national policies. Better mechanisms are needed for the transfer of basic knowledge to applications, and vice versa, because coping with very practical problems can invigorate basic science.

GOVERNMENT/SCIENCE RELATIONS

Budgetary policy for science and technology has for a long time been incremental, and segmented by disciplines and governmental sectors. Especially in a small country, but apparently also for large nations, this is no longer satisfactory.

Many and sometimes confusing attempts are made to direct research in socially useful directions, by offering scientists incentives and restrictions, as a substitute for their own professional judgement. At the same time assumptions are made about the potential practical use of R & D for the private sector by offering incentives (subsidies, research facilities), in some cases as a substitute for the commercial judgement of the entrepreneurs.

Especially in organizations with the promotion of basic research as their principal objective, a gap is manifest between results of research and the practical utilization thereof in the public or private domain. There are several endeavours to compensate for this gap, as well as to try to implant in the research programme a greater orientation towards societal needs, with programmes for problem-orientated or strategic research. In some cases potential users of the programme can be involved from the start, but even then, much effort is needed to make the information accessible to all those potentially interested. The development of strategies and mechanisms for the stimulation of investment in R & D, and for the acceleration of the introduction of new technologies in the private and in the public sector, is an important item on the agenda of national science policy everywhere. The experiments range from specific projects to facilitating contract research in public laboratories and universities and to public–private joint ventures in research programmes or the initiation of research centres.

PRIORITIES

Crucial in the problem of setting priorities for research is the need to satisfy intrinsic and extrinsic criteria; that is for important conceptual advances in basic research and contributions to other fields of research and for potential applicability to urgent social, infrastructural (including environmental) and economic problems.

Within fields, priorities are usually set mainly through a combination of intrinsic criteria and extrinsic criteria put forth by scientists, agency administrators, civil servants and interest groups in documents prepared by a variety of advisory bodies. Priorities across fields of research have been set only implicitly or not at all.

Priority-setting exercises have for some time been rewarded by extra public finances to stimulate particular areas without harming others. Increasing budget constraints, but also an increasing political commitment to science and technology as a condition to sustain welfare and economic competition, have changed this. More emphasis is put on potential use of the results of R & D with regard to urgent societal problems.

In The Netherlands, as in most other countries, two driving priorities are struggling for the prominent position: cutting public expenditure and stimulating economic growth (and thereby employment). All public activities are reexamined with regard to these priorities — also expenditures on research and development. On the one hand science and technology are seen as the key to economic growth and the sustaining of basic living conditions; on the other hand government realizes its role is limited, not only for budgetary reasons, but also because government lacks adequate insight as to what knowledge might have the potential for practical use and can be used by commercial enterprises.

Some experience is now available for national and supranational surveys concerning the health and orientation of major fields of science. In general a thorough survey conducted by prominent scientists is accepted by the scientific community, but surveys have limitations as a mechanism to provide information to policymakers for setting priorities, partly because of insufficient orientation toward social problems or agency missions. Another limitation is that surveys are easier to conduct for coherent disciplines with large-scale instrumentation and facility needs than for new areas and dispersed science fields that are not organized to share expensive facilities.

THE EXPLOITATION OF KNOWLEDGE

There are three main reasons for the public support of R & D: (1) support of basic science for its intellectual value and for the education of scientists and professionals; (2) to carry out specific missions (safety, health, environment); and (3) to further economic well-being. Any kind of research may respond to one or more of these goals, but the role of government differs in each case. The most important role for government is probably in the procurement of knowledge and tools it needs for conducting its own specific public tasks: administration, health care, environmental and infrastructural responsibilities. Self-reliance in all aspects of a nation's needs is not a feasible target for a small country like The Netherlands, but in some respects our specific struggle with nature has made us strong, for instance in water-management, civil engineering and marine technology.

The fact that we cannot do everything must not prevent us from doing what is most important: priorities must be set. Government procurement can play a crucial role here, possibly combined with efforts to commercialize the resulting knowledge and techniques. Advanced technical needs in the public sector can be a very powerful instrument in fostering innovation. One has to consider making the new technology available to all potential users versus giving exclusive rights to specific enterprises.

On the one hand a government can be blamed for not furthering the maximum exploitation of the technology promoted for specific use; on the other hand giving privileges to some and excluding others is inconsistent with the principle of equity. Of course criteria for judging this are different for different stages, from fundamental research to developmental activities. Fundamental theoretical research requires an unrestricted and international scientific discussion. This holds for institutions whose main task it is to do fundamental and strategic research, as well as for the education of scientists and professionals. Universities or members of the staff can however take part in consortia or perform contract research as long as their primary scientific task does not depend on this and realistic costing takes place.

THE CASE OF AGRICULTURAL RESEARCH

In The Netherlands agricultural research and education and transfer of knowledge are associated in an exemplary way. This is supposed to be the main reason that The Netherlands is one of the biggest exporters of value-added agricultural products. Science, applied science, technology and training are combined in a system for coupling knowledge with the people who will apply it in the field. For a long time the speciality has been empirical genetics, but technical knowledge about mechanization, crop specialization and all kinds of know-how and logistic support systems are regionally brought together. This system remained continuously innovative, representing the paradigm of conditions that are essential for innovative productive science.

However, trying to transpose this system of generation and diffusion of knowledge to other sectors makes clear that the agricultural sector is unique because of its economic structure. It consists of small enterprises, too small to take care of their own research. These enterprises do not act as competitors but assemble to solve collective problems. At the same time the supply-side of research collaborates strongly with the educational system and in transferring knowledge to the farmers. The transfer of knowledge does not seem to be a problem here, the farmers constantly pose their problems to the scientists and tend to use applications immediately. In small industry in other sectors this is not the case: competition there hinders small and medium enterprises in striving for collective research.

THE INSTITUTIONAL FACTOR

There is reason to argue that current institutional structure and management arrangements for science impede close links between science and applications. Performing excellent basic research in elite universities, and in some public and industrial laboratories, and having a good record in immediate product development in some fields do not save us from being weak at the parts of the process that lie in-between. We can easily observe a lack of sophistication and intelligent management of the path from science to innovation. One of the causes for this is the tendency to treat basic research in a vacuum, while in many cases it should be regarded as one of the components of our effort that leads to the solution of the larger problems of society: health care, environmental conditions, poverty, industrial decline and unemployment, to name but a few. In our institutional arrangements we must be aware of the interconnectedness of basic research with other parts of the process — with applied science, with engineering and technology, with public, national needs. What we require is purposive or strategic basic research of a fundamental nature that is done with a general application in view, as is the case in most biomedical research. Purposive basic research, applied science and engineering are critical in the utilization of scientific discoveries and often will lead to major scientific advances. There are many examples to demonstrate that historically the arrow of causality is from the technology to the science, instead of the other way round. It need not be true that applied research drives out pure research. Look at how the computer has changed mathematical science, biology and even the behavioural sciences and the humanities. The successes in biotechnology are partly a result of cross-disciplinary work, engineering as much as biology.

From where do we expect relevant new knowledge to come? Industry, by nature, has to take a relatively short-term view of what products are needed. Private non-profit institutions hardly exist any more. Government must shape the conditions for new knowledge in its own laboratories and in the universities, the best place for knowledge to increase.

Can we trust government to do this? Many complain that applied science policy is in some respects inadequate and disruptive. Governments may start and stop applied science and development programmes too hastily, while handing out scarce funds to scattered groups. As a result the applied science that is performed is often fragmented and inadequately linked to basic research and the education of university students, and eventually can damage good basic research.

On the other hand the administration of basic research is characterized by a weak management style that is inadequate for dealing with applied projects. We argue that the public applied science infrastructure is invaluable for the orderly transformation of pure knowledge into societal and economic value.

The above reasoning leads to the conclusion that each part of the spectrum from undirected basic research, purposive basic research, applied science, engineering and technology should be given equal weight and their essential interdependence should be stressed, as well as the interconnectedness of disciplines and institutions.

We must be willing to analyse our situation objectively, to have a close look at the institutional structure and funding arrangements and have the courage to experiment with alternatives. Industry–university partnerships and the use of state-of-the-art knowledge by agencies with public missions must be encouraged.

INDUSTRIAL RESEARCH AND THE MANAGEMENT OF SCIENCE

Support of basic research will not automatically lead to societal benefits via public or industrial applications. We can fail to use the basic research performed in universities and laboratories because we lack the appropriate industry that can take advantage of it and because we lack the infrastructure that is needed to close the gap between basic research and applications.

New products and production techniques are the results of technological developments. The support of technological developments for commercial purposes is best left with private industry. In industrial R & D results are used from fundamental research in universities and fundamental and applied research in national research laboratories. The responsibility for this science infrastructure is best left with the government, in line with the responsibility for more general societal concerns, as welfare and other conditions for economic well-being, such as adequate infrastructural facilities. The transfer of ideas from universities and laboratories to industry and vice versa is of great importance and a concern of both. The fast dissemination of new techniques is of great interest to all sectors of the society and the economy.

The transfer of knowledge and technology should take place in active partnership between fundamental and application-orientated scientists. For this, university–industrial collaboration in strategic research is needed. The provision of venture capital to scientist-entrepreneurs and the establishment of research parks and information centres for small businesses are popular instruments, but do not fully answer this need.

Within industry the gulf between basic and applied science makes itself felt as well. The industrial scientist may have an attitude analogous to that of his academic colleagues, and the work in research divisions may be looked at as a separate ivory tower activity. When times get tough industry will cut back on research, as will national governments.

A weakness in industry's management of science could be that industry managers increasingly lose touch with science and technology, while at the same time many of the management's decisions are of a technological nature. Nevertheless it is obvious that industrial organizations can have good basic science and innovate at the same time.

An example of this synergism in industry is set by Philips. Here is one of the instances where industry has fostered basic research when others gave up long-term projects. The position of agriculture illustrates that even government can contribute to the process that enables a research system to stay innovative over a long period.

There is need for strong interconnections between industry, universities and government laboratories for long-term applied research. In this respect the formula used in the United States for setting up, with the help of the National Science Foundation, Science and Technology Centres, could prove successful. In these centres academic and industrial researchers work on promising areas, and a number of companies and academic institutions are members.

THE HUMAN FACTOR

Our concern is not only with the orientation but also with the productivity of the science profession. Doing research has become burdened with administrative tasks, procedural rituals and government regulation. A system is needed to enable scientists to concentrate on their scientific work and public service.

Despite the massive scale of the research system, real cutting-edge science is only done by a limited number of organizations with very talented people, a critical mass of related research and very advanced instrumentation. These institutions demonstrate that science should be run from below, but strong managers are needed to establish linkages and fend off governmental or other interferences. It is imperative, however, that the science community not become isolated from the larger problems of the country. The profession itself should help to overcome the gaps that separates science from management, government and the public at large. The potential that advances in knowledge can offer should be regarded as a concern for everyone. The more attractive science becomes for practical or commercial use, the more the profession will need to make responsible judgements about when human welfare, ethics, environmental standards or academic freedom are compromised.

NEW INTERNATIONAL AND SOCIETAL FACTORS

One of the current paradoxes is that in some ways the climate for international cooperation in science is better than ever before, but in other respects the climate worsens. Governments and businesses try to win the global race and this leads to strong pressures to stop communication of scientific information. Although there is a need for bringing together basic and applied science there is the problem that the line is difficult to draw between what information must be free and what can be restricted. All investors, whether governments or industry, want the best science as well as the highest economic value from their investment. This leaves us all with the same adaptive problem, for which there is no easy solution. Besides international competition we all see changes in the environment and new needs: values and lifestyles change, the domestic and the global economy stagnates, there are changes in the demography and the transition to an information and service-dominated society. We can ask ourselves what this means when we discuss what should be done to maximize the intellectual and practical contribution of science.

Let us highlight some of the problems that confront us.

— Much has been achieved by governments, but much more purposeful research is needed to achieve good living conditions: a safe environment and good health for everyone, good high-speed transport, economical energy sources and utilization, safe buildings and many other needs in public sectors.
— National basic science systems struggle with deep structural problems that hinder productivity.
— University research talent could be better used. Morale often is low, there is an undue fixation on funding trends and much energy is dissipated. Contract research is taken on to stay alive, and does not contribute to partnership and reorientation. Freedom from the 'dead hand of bureaucracy' is needed.
— Governmental science institutions and policies are not sufficiently successful in bringing together basic and applied science in fruitful collaboration.
— Sudden affections of governments for 'the market' can lead to neglect and unhealthy instability in science organizations.
— Industry suffers as well from some of the problems governments have.
— The science profession is not sufficiently aware of its responsibilities towards general science education, public service and ethical matters.
— The results of fundamental research are by nature an international good. Many applications based on that knowledge become industrial or national property. The resulting tension will stay with us. The science profession will have to stand up for a free flow of knowledge.

7 The Indian scene

Sukh Dev

INTRODUCTION

Manufacturing and agriculture are important sectors of any developed economy. One of the key factors responsible for the prosperity and well-being of most of the population in Europe, North America and Japan has been the systematic application of science to upgrade their agriculture and manufacturing activity and capability Thus, for a developing economy it is essential to strengthen this capability, both in qualitative and quantitative terms, not only to satisfy its internal demand but also to contribute to its export trade in a significant manner.

There are two mechanisms by which a developing country can enlarge and strengthen its industrial and agricultural base. These are: (a) import of technology and (b) indigenous generation of technology through R & D. Both mechanisms have their validity depending upon the particulars of a situation. Obviously, there is no point in rediscovering the wheel, and one cannot afford to lose time. Thus, in the first phase import of technology will be a must to achieve quickly a certain capability both in manufacturing and infrastructure. Up to this point the required technologies would be competitively available and on reasonable terms. The present industrial boom of countries like South Korea and Taiwan is essentially from technology imports. More than 75 per cent of electronic goods, 70 per cent of agricultural machinery, 65 per cent of transport machinery, almost all petrochemical and fertilizer production, and some 35 per cent of drugs and pharmaceuticals made in India are products of imported technology.[1,2,3] However, as a nation moves towards more specialized items or so-called 'high-tech' areas, especially those covering defence requirements, imported technologies are just not for sale. Moreover, in some cases, the terms of technology import may not be compatible with the political aspirations of the country. Above all, as a nation moves towards a developed economy, it becomes imperative both from fiscal and political considerations, that the country should have acquired the capability to generate and export technologies. This is a prime requirement for large countries like India, if they wish to stand with some dignity in the community of nations. Thus, under all these situations, indigenous generation of technology through R & D becomes a must. Such an R & D base is also essential for assimilating and improving on imported technology, and assists in judicious selection of imported technology.

INDIA'S SCIENCE AND TECHNOLOGY BASE

India has built up, over the years, a respectable R & D base.[1,4,5] India has 150 universities and five Institutes of Technology which turn out approximately 100,000 diploma holders, graduates and postgraduates in various science and engineering disciplines every year. The current economically active science and technology people number about 3 million. Current out-turn of doctorates in science and related subjects is some 4,000 per year. Every year Indian scientists and research workers publish over 20,000 research papers, accounting for about 3 per cent of global output per year.

The total number of research institutions engaged in R & D work is about 1,300. These come under the purview of various agencies of central government, state government, public-sector undertakings and the private sector. For 1985–6 R & D expenditure has been estimated at Rs.21,800 million, which comes to about 0.94 per cent of India's GNP. For international comparison it may be mentioned that R & D expenditures of the United States and the Soviet Union for the same period were approximately 2.7 per cent and 4.7 per cent of GNP respectively.[6] Of the total expenditure on R & D in India, the outlay by the central government, state government and private sector were respectively 78 per cent, 9 per cent and 13 per cent. Table 7.1 depicts R & D expenditure broken down by sector.

Table 7.1   R & D expenditure for various economy sectors 1985–6 (%)

Sector	Percentage allocation
Agriculture, forestry and fisheries	17.9
Manufacturing	17.8
Energy	16.8
Defence	15.4
Space	9.3
Transport, communications	5.2
Basic research	4.3
Others	13.3

Source: Research & Development Statistics (1984–1985), Government of India, Dept. of Science and Technology.

Total scientific and technical manpower engaged in R & D is around 94,000 putting India in ninth place at the international level in this respect.

IMPACT OF R & D ACTIVITY ON DIFFERENT SECTORS OF THE INDIAN ECONOMY

Against this background, one would now like to survey, very briefly, important areas of economic activity which have profitably drawn on indigenous R & D for growth.[1,5,7,8] Some sectors which have essentially failed to take advantage of R & D in a meaningful manner are also listed. The only criterion used in this evaluation is the extent to which the R & D effort has helped in the country's economic growth.

Agriculture in India has benefited considerably from indigenous R & D. The apex agency for all agricultural and related research in the country is the Indian Council of Agricultural Research (ICAR), which has a large number of research institutes (over forty-five) under its direct jurisdiction. The main thrust of this agency's activity has been directed at crop management. A large number of varieties of rice, wheat, maize, etc. for cultivation in various agro-climatic regions of the country were developed and released to farmers. The net result has been the transformation from a food-deficient country to a self-sufficient one. Although this is very significant, much remains to be done as the yields per hectare for many crops such as rice, cotton, groundnuts, etc. are still much below that achieved by others.

Another success story is that of atomic energy, which comes under the purview of the department of atomic energy (DAE). The atomic energy programme has, as its objective, the generation of electrical power from nuclear energy and production of radio-isotopes for research and medicine. The first atomic power plant (Tarapur, 1964) was purchased on a turn-key basis. The second plant (Unit I of the Rajasthan atomic power station) had a high imported material component, while Unit II of the Rajasthan atomic power station has been essentially built locally. Today India is among the seven or eight countries to have expertise in the complete fuel cycle. The radio-isotopes produced at Bhabha Atomic Research Centre (BARC) are not only meeting internal demand but are also being exported. However, much remains to be achieved. After over thirty years of the creation of the DAE, the total installed capacity of power is only 1,330 MW. Projects have been taking over twelve years for completion.

India has acquired considerable capability in the area of space technology, which is crucial for communication, remote sensing, meteorology and defence. The department of space (DOS), the executive wing of the Space Commission, was established in 1972. It has several institutes under its control. The space programme had valuable spin-offs. Some eighty technologies developed by its R & D wing, the Indian Space Research Organization (ISRO), have been transferred to industry, of which some seventy are in production.

A fine organic chemicals industry is crucial to modern society as it comprises pharmaceuticals (for health care), pesticides (for agriculture, public health, etc.), aroma chemicals (for soaps, detergents, cosmetics), dyes, pigments, food additives, etc. Table 7.2 shows India's production and imports, and production as a percentage of total requirements (1985–6). From this it is evident that indigenous production contributes, to a large extent, towards meeting the country's requirements. Some of these products are being exported as well. Most of the R & D effort in this area has come from laboratories of the CSIR and private R & D establishments.

The examples cited so far clearly indicate the benefits which have accrued to the nation from the R & D system. However, there are

Table 7.2 Production and imports of certain fine organic chemicals, 1985–6
          (in Crores[+] of Rs)

Class	Production	Imports	Production as % of total
Drugs (bulk)[10]	410.0	20.0	93
Pesticides (technical)[9]	420.0 (66,440 tonnes)	5.0 (947 tonnes)	99
Dyestuffs[10]	200.0* (18,745 tonnes)	10.5	95
Aroma chemicals and essential oils[10]	100.0*	20.0*	83

[+] 1 Crore = 10 million
* Estimated.

several vital areas where indigenous R & D has scarcely made any impact. Some of these are:

Petrochemicals
Polymers and plastics
Synthetic fibres
Fertilizers
Fermentation technology, including antibiotics
Industrial enzymes
Advanced materials
Electronics

Moreover, whatever achievements have been presented above are essentially products of development work, where research has played only a minor role. Products, processes, techniques, basic knowledge had been known, and all that was done was to draw on this resource for doing a particular job in a known fashion. Our contributions during the post-independence period towards the generation of new products and new processes, which calls for a high level of research component, have been essentially negligible.

Thus, the overall performance of the R & D system in India, at best, has been mediocre. In the meantime, the so-called developed countries have continued to develop at a rate and in a direction of technology development that has outstripped the industrial growth of developing countries like India. It then becomes imperative that one takes a hard look at India's R & D system, which certainly is one of the crucial means for developing an independent and buoyant economy.

PREREQUISITES FOR EFFECTIVE R & D

R & D provides the mechanism to convert scientific knowledge and information, old and new, into something tangible for society. The driving force for R & D is economic advantage, while governments often also invest funds in R & D for purely social purposes or security reasons. Thus, the final outcome of any R & D effort must be measurable in economic terms. There are several factors which have come to be recognized as important for the success of R & D outlays, and these are briefly discussed below.

Infrastructure in terms of manpower, physical assets and facilities, and organizational set-up must be adequate. Given sufficient numbers in any sphere of activity, a few people will excel. However, unless the base level is high enough, productivity will suffer. Unfortunately, in India much remains to be accomplished in science teaching and research, and urgent steps are required to rectify this to improve the quality. Though most of the R & D establishments are adequately equipped and housed, maintenance of equipment at optimum level appears to be inadequate. The general infrastructure is also poor. Proper power supply, water supply, communication (phones, telex, etc.) go a long way in ensuring good productivity. Effective organizational set-up can be most important. This becomes clear from the fact that Indians' performance, when working in Western countries, is invariably superior to what they are able to accomplish at home.

PROJECT IDENTIFICATION

Why R & D? Is it not ultimately for the benefit of the people? If so, then before thrust areas/projects for R & D inputs are identified, it should be considered essential to identify the needs of the country in concrete terms. To do this it will first be necessary to select a model for the society, which need not necessarily be based on consumerism — a culture pressurizing people to work hard to meet their ever-increasing real and imaginary demands. 'Perfection of means and confusion of goals' has been described as the characteristic of our age by Albert Einstein.[11] Having identified the needs, these should be broken down into clear-cut projects. The sharper the recognition of the problem, the greater are the chances of a project's success. Manufacturing activity often throws up problems which can be converted into economic opportunities. Basic research, on the other hand, produces seeds of technology, which must be recognized. Hence a vigorous interaction between academia and industry is called for and is ideal for exploiting such situations. German and Japanese science are characterized by this symbiosis. In India, unfortunately, this is almost totally lacking.

Having identified the problem/project, the correct strategy must be selected. It has been stated that 'there is no orderly method that can be prescribed to make a discovery or to perform any other creative act'.[12] This is quite true when we talk of basic discoveries. Dedication, capacity to concentrate deeply, imagination, intuition, flashes of insight and a deep understanding of the problem appear to be some of the traits of these scientists and inventors. However for market-driven research, systematic approaches to creative action have been devised[13] which consciously or unconsciously may be familiar to many involved in creative activity. Of these, the uninhibited approach to thinking — brainstorming — appears to be most popular. In all this, a clear and concise definition of the problem, excellent knowledge of the background literature and a good analytical mind will go a long way in planning an effective strategy. Serendipity has often played an important role in discoveries, but Prince Serendip assists those who work with a receptive mind, open eyes and have a broad comprehension!

The next step would be adequate resources to complete the job in a reasonable time-frame. Time is a crucial factor. The objective should be to complete the job as early as possible, without sacrificing quality or attention to details, so that the project starts yielding economic returns. In my experience, though in the relatively restricted field of fine organic chemicals, I have felt that our outlay in terms of effective manpower for most projects in our national laboratories, tends to be totally inadequate. This results in the project being dragged on for years, whereupon the project itself loses all relevance.

All work, all ideas are carried out ultimately by human beings. Thus, the most crucial factor besides personnel quality is personnel motivation. Unless the people involved take the project as a personal challenge and give it their best, no amount of planning will ever succeed. There are people who are intrinsically dedicated and hard-working. But such numbers are small. Others must be motivated. The more people are involved in planning and decisionmaking, the greater their motivation. Nothing works better than the possibility of financial benefit and recognition. Employee–inventors should be entitled to royalty payments on their products and processes, or other means should be found to reward the work.

Finally, government policies play a paramount role in the success of the R & D system. Government policies should be clear, well-defined, should be formulated on a long-term basis and should be geared to the strengthening of the indigenous R & D capability and productivity. Tariff structure should be such as to encourage raw material import and discourage raw material export; on the other hand high tariffs should be levied on penultimate stage goods or intermediates. In India no fixed policy appears to be operating in this regard. Tariff structure is often changed to suit certain groups with political influence. The government should clearly decide on technologies to be imported and those to be developed indigenously, keeping in view the immediate needs and future perspective. The main reason for the success of our atomic energy and space programmes has been the clear mandate (for whatever reason) given to these agencies so that a mission-orientated programme could be carried out. Our failure on the petrochemical side has been essentially due to lack of such a determination, otherwise one sees no reason why expansion of petrochemical capacity (at other locations) could not be carried out indigenously after the initial import of technology. Too many international hawkers trying to sell their wares to India through various means (often dubious), have essentially come in the way of generating our own capability in this area. Such an international situation does not prevail in the atomic energy and space sectors. If one has to name a single factor which has helped the Indian pharmaceutical and pesticide industries to achieve their present state of development, it is the enactment of new patent law — The Patents Act, 1970[14] — which does not recognize a chemical entity, but only protects its process of manufacture, and that for only a rather limited period. Of course, this has had a deleterious effect on the capability of our drug and pesticide industries to generate new molecules for drugs and pesticides. However, the overall impact has been beneficial to the country. Recently, the United States modified its laws to permit transfer of technology from government laboratories to private-sector entrepreneurs including exclusive rights to the patents.[15] This has resulted in greater commercialization of such technologies. Providing R & D incentives, risk venture capital, equity participation by government agencies, tax benefits, high-technology parks, etc. are other ways to encourage generation and utilization of indigenous technology.

CONCLUSIONS

(1) India's performance in utilizing indigenously generated technologies has been mixed. The system has worked best whenever a clearly defined mission has been undertaken.
(2) India's performance in generating new products and new processes has been poor.
(3) Government regulations have played an important role, both positive and negative.

NOTES

1. *Status Report on Science and Technology in India: 1986*, CSIR, New Delhi (1986).
2. N.C. Mehta in *Perspective Plan for Petrochemicals*, Proceedings of the Seminar organized by ICMA, New Delhi, May 1978, p. 25, Indian Chemical Manufacturers Association, Calcutta (1978).
3. *Chemical Weekly*, Annual Number (15 August 1988), p. 137.
4. *Research & Development Statistics (1984–1985)*, Government of India, Dept. of Science and Technology.
5. *Statistical Outline of India (1988–1989)*, Tata Services, Dept. of Economics and Statistics, Bombay (1988).
6. *Statistical Year Book (1985)*, UNESCO, Paris.
7. S.K. Mukerji and B.V. Subbarayappa (eds), *Science in India: A Changing Profile*, Indian National Science Academy, New Delhi (1984).
8. *National Science Day: A Commemorative Volume*, CSIR, New Delhi (1987).
9. *40 Years of Research: A CSIR Overview*, CSIR, New Delhi (1988).
10. Chemical Weekly, op. cit., p. 209.
11. Quoted in *Chemical Technology*, 11 (1981), 590.
12. Nobel Laureate Peter Medawar quoted in *Machine Design*, 50, No. 10, (1978).

13. W.G. Hyzer, *Industrial Research & Development*, **143** (Sept. 1978).
14. *Gazette of India Extraordinary*, Part II (Section I), Sept. 1970; also see R.B. Pai, *Journal of Scientific and Industrial Research*, **29** (1970), 483.
15. R.R. Jones, *Research & Development*, **74** (April, 1988).

8 The relationship between scientific research and technological innovation

F. Prakke

ON GENERAL PRINCIPLES OF MANAGING R & D SYSTEMS

In recent years there has been a development in the thinking about the principles of managing goal-orientated science which is pertinent to the practical use of the results of R & D systems. Such principles of managing science seem equally applicable to industrial and government R & D, and to a wide variety of national and cultural contexts. These principles concern the relationship between scientific research and technological innovation, two key elements of any goal-orientated R & D system, and the type of management (or policy) interventions that are most likely to improve the quality of that R & D system.

The traditional thinking, dominant in the decades following the Second World War, holds that there is a causal chain that starts with basic research and ends in technological advances, or innovation (see Figure 8.1), i.e. successful application to some social need or introduction on the market.

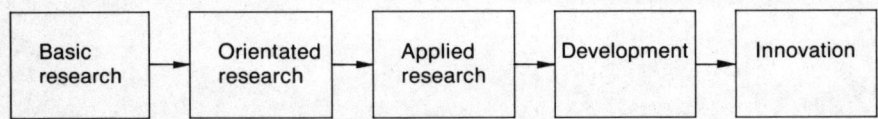

Figure 8.1   Traditional causal chain of the R & D process

This has long been a very popular view of progress in science and technology. The reason is the apparent logic of such a causal chain. It seems evident and logical that technological breakthroughs of modern times are in some way building on previous scientific discoveries. The management principles that were drawn from this model of technological progress were that it was sufficient to maintain high-quality basic research and to make intelligible choices with respect to orientated research. From there innovation would follow almost automatically. Great Britain has had the experience that this approach to managing a national R & D system produces many Nobel laureates, but poor international competitiveness.

Retrospective research on innovation has produced the conclusion that innovation is based on basic scientific research only in a very roundabout and lengthy way. Sherwin and Isenson (1967) found no instance of innovations in military hardware in the 1960s based on basic scientific knowledge less than twenty years old. Project TRACES found that the modal age of basic research findings that contributed to fifteen major innovations was between twenty and thirty years. A number of different studies of the time lag between the availability of information and a consequent innovation have shown this to be a period of many years in several different industries. This is especially, but not exclusively, true of the major innovations. Studies of diffusion, a special and very important part of the total innovation process, have shown that after an innovation has first been successfully put in use, it often takes many years before most of an industry accepts it (Mansfield, 1961).

Such data also show that it is not logical to separate diffusion from the concept of innovation, especially if we are interested — as we usually are — in the impact of innovation on such goals as industrial productivity and general economic welfare. From the standpoint of industrial efficiency, at least, we are much more interested in broad technological progress than in spectacular individual advances. It has been computed, in OECD countries, that the most productive enterprises in an industry often lead their competitors in productivity by a factor of two or three, and that increasing the productivity of the backward firms to the industry average would raise the productivity of the entire industry by about 100 per cent. While such computations are based on necessarily imperfect measures, the clear implication is, again, that scientific performance is not the critical factor in innovative performance. High-quality scientific research is perhaps a necessary but not a sufficient condition for producing technological progress.

I would be willing to argue that for many R & D systems the causal chain of performance actually runs in exactly the opposite direction: from market innovation via applied research to basic research.

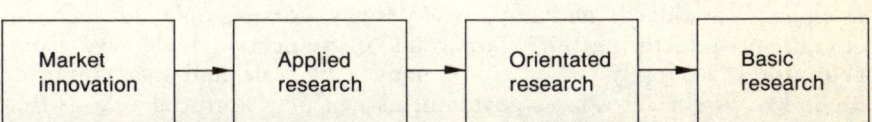

Figure 8.2   Inverted causal chain of the R & D process

Support for this view comes from recent changes in industrial R & D management in large European firms. Many firms have moved away from centralized, science-orientated R & D laboratories toward decentralized R & D, directly responsible to product divisions and orientated toward market demand. Moreover, the Dutch agricultural R & D system provides an example of research primarily influenced by demand. A highly sophisticated marketing and distribution system produces signals about the desirability of changes in farm products. This leads to demands for consultants, extension services and particular types of applied research at the local level. Unsolved problems are passed on to 'orientated' and 'basic' research groups at the agricultural university of Wageningen. The quality of the linkages between the actors in this chain determines the innovative performance.

More sophisticated treatments of these relationships than offered by this admittedly crude 'inverted causal chain' approach can be found in the literature on diffusion and utilization of knowledge (for example, Wolek, 1984; Rogers, Eveland and Bean, 1976). The management principles to be drawn from this are that research institutes should be orientated toward and made dependent on actors in the R & D system closer to final demand, particularly advanced users. Orientation based solely on scientific prestige should be avoided.

THREE TYPES OF TECHNOLOGICAL CHANGE

Changes in the nature of technology itself support stressing user orientation in the management of national R & D systems. The technologies that are dominant in the 1980s in terms of technological opportunity and impact on society are different from those of thirty years ago. They require different policy approaches. This can be argued in the following way. Three types of technological change can be identified, depending on the kind of obstacles to progress that are met and on the kind of design options that are typical. Technological change is either research orientated, design orientated or application orientated. Examples of research-orientated technological change are speciality chemicals and pharmaceuticals. Once a breakthrough in research has taken place, approach to the market is rather straightforward. Specialized research scientists and well-equipped laboratories determine the success of the innovation process, much as in Figure 8.1. Design-orientated technological change is typical of transportation equipment, aerospace and computer hardware. Scientific knowledge on which the design is based is either rather stable or readily available to many competitors. Success depends on solving technical design problems, usually based on contributions from several disciplines. Standards and dominant designs (for example the DC-3 in aircraft manufacturing) are important instruments of change. Competitiveness is closely linked to economies of scale and manufacturing capability. As in aerospace, governments can play a crucial role as first user.

A third type of technological change is application orientated. The most important obstacles are neither in research nor in the design. Delay and (mis)direction in the application of technical possibilities lie in local application. Agriculture is traditionally an area in which technological progress is strongly dependent on local circumstances such as the provision of extension services, demonstration farms, consultants and the education level of the farmers. Not only obstacles but also the direction of the technical developments are determined locally. Depending on local culture, power relationships, or degree of organization, different applications evolve. Present developments in the area of factory automation and all information technology seem to be determined locally (Prakke, 1986). Application-orientated technologies are typically 'managed' by instruments like demonstration projects and the creation of new social networks, rather than R & D project selection.

In conclusion, one can say that technical development can mainly be determined and directed either in the research phase, in the design phase or in the application phase. The present dominance of information technology, which belongs to the third category, means that in the 1980s other innovation and diffusion mechanisms are more important than those of forty years ago when developments in petrochemicals and transportation equipment were dominant. In information technology a relatively large role seems to be played by small-scale entrepreneurs who are able to exploit market niches and operate in symbiosis with advanced users. An analogous conclusion is drawn by FAST, the European Community programme for 'Forecasting and Assessment of Science and Technology'. It states that 'user orientation' is of crucial importance in the development of information-technology-related areas such as the service-sector, telecommunication and automation. This is certainly a shift from traditional science policy concerns. Perhaps the most important lesson to be drawn is that science policy must change with the times. It cannot afford to be orientated solely on scientific disciplines. It should rather start from an analysis of changes in societal needs with respect to dominant scientific opportunities.

CONCLUSION

The following issues with regard to science policy implementation can be singled out from the discussion above.

(1) Scientific advance is dependent on close linkages to advanced users. It should be the role of science policy to foster such linkages. Such linkages often develop into complex networks, encompassing consulting and training as well as scientific research, as in the agricultural system in The Netherlands. The strength of these networks is determined by the weakest link. West Germany, Japan and Taiwan are examples of countries that have developed strong networks in the area of industrial technology.

(2) R & D systems must be made responsive to changes in demand for their services. The new technologies require different management approaches. Flexibility is more important than the optimalization of project selection procedures.

(3) Entrepreneurship is an important element in the progress of such new areas as information technology (IT) and biotechnology. Science policy must learn to make use of market forces and competition to enrich the national R & D system. Universities must encourage small-scale advanced entrepreneurs in their direct environment to achieve mutual benefits. Such entrepreneurs serve as instruments of technology transfer as well as generators of relevant research problems.

(4) Advances in information technology are typically the result not of laboratory research but of experimentation by users in a real-life context. Typical science policy instruments for IT are therefore demonstration projects and social stereotyping.

REFERENCES

Mansfield, E., 'Technical change and the rate of imitation', *Econometrics*, October 1961.
Prakke, F., 'Manufacturing innovation between the state and the market', in A. Gerstenfeld, H.J. Bullinger and H.J. Warnecke (eds), *Manufacturing research: Organizational and Institutional Issues*, Amsterdam, Elsevier Science Publishers, 1986.
Rogers, E.M., Eveland, J.D., Bean, A.S., 'Extending the agricultural extension model', Institute for Communication Research, Stanford University, 1976.
Sherwin, C.W. and Isenson, R.S., 'Project Hindsight, a defense department study of the utility of research', *Science*, June 1967.
Wolek, F.W., 'Technology transfer', Wharton School, University of Pennsylvania, 1984.

Discussion summary

A.D. Wolff-Albers

While the prepared papers successively concentrated on the principal role of government, and on the impact (or lack of impact) of R & D on different sectors in the Indian economy, the discussion extended to favourable and hampering conditions for the exploitation of new knowledge. A vital factor in order to appreciate the value of available knowledge was pointed out: the sender and the receiver (the potential user) should be on each other's wavelength and the receiver must have adequate expertise. Enlarging on the concept of sender and receiver, a 'transmitter' is needed. India as a whole is a very large receiver, with specific requirements. Some technologies are good, but others can be too expensive or polluting. However, it was also noted that the model of sender/receiver was too simple to give a complete picture. It neglects practical or material impediments to the use of science such as lack of data, scientific journals, necessary chemicals etc.

It was observed that diffusion of knowledge is unlike diffusion of technology. In science there is free exchange of information, the exchange of know-how in technology is more restricted and subject to patent policy. Japan absorbs at science level and brings the knowledge to technology level. This demonstrates that you need not be brilliant in science to be good in technology (Italy), or you may have a weak industry but be good in science (United Kingdom). It was argued that basic research may be the prime mover for new applicable knowledge, but not always. It is conventional to think that there is a forceful chain from discovery to application and use, but the other way round is often more in accordance with what really happens. As a counter example genetic engineering was mentioned, where new varieties only come through basic research, as for example Japan is apparently aware. It was also requested that a distinction be made between enhancement in R & D as such and in R & D from production units.

As several discussants pointed out attention needs to be focused on the social and environmental consequences attendant on the introduction of technologies; there governments definitely have an important task. These consequences can be seen as costs of technology in a wider sense — which can turn out to be too high. A related difficulty is that the indirect benefits and spinoffs from science and technology cannot easily be quantified. In The Netherlands at the request of Parliament a special organization for technology assessment was set up.

In the area of government intervention some of the Indian experience was discussed. As for the use of 'missions' a useful distinction can be made between purely organizational missions and R & D missions to generate knowledge. The situation for bringing R & D to practical use certainly varies:

— if the public mission coincides with public R & D. The adequate allotment of research money is a problem. When cuts are necessary, some government sectors cut research first which in essence is very irrational;
— if government provides the infrastructure, but does not act as a customer (agriculture, health);
— if government has to provide linkage of public R & D with the private sector. This category is considered the most complicated.

In fact, the matter of practical use of research is not only dependent on the system of private production, but also on the pubic sector. CSIR research cuts across all sectors (aeronautics to sanitation). The question is how to divide resources and how to enhance utility. At the same time a need for clarification of the role of certain instruments was felt: what incentives can be given to use knowledge and what is the role of the government towards industry? Given the ability of the government to decide what knowledge can have practical results, there remain questions about commercial government procurement, and the matter of exclusive use of public knowledge.

In looking at the Dutch experience with government intervention, it was put forward as the government's first responsibility to invest in good education and in research at international level. Government needs science and technology in order to perform public tasks, and in this respect it can play the role of the leading-edge customer. In this respect joint ventures between industry and government and the scientific community can be successful. In general, governments will try to assist entrepreneurs, sometimes in an indirect way by, for example, setting standards for health care and pollution. Examples were given of specific activities by the Dutch government. An old example is the aeronautical sector: there education, the mission-orientated laboratory (the National Aeronautical Laboratory) and industry are all in tune. In this case there is an explicit government policy to spend money on the aircraft industry. Other traditional examples are agriculture and water management (Delta works). A very active innovation policy has been conducted in The Netherlands from the seventies onwards in fields such as biotechnology, new materials and computer science. As can be expected the evaluation of the policies differs from case to case, and differs largely for generic technology and specific technology and with the structural aspects of the sector concerned.

In general the discussion provoked no controversy on principles, but evoked an unmistakable interest in tools, in effective policies and practical experiences in initiating the use of R & D in both countries, including patent policies. It became clear that there can be inconsistencies between principles and practice. It must, however, be understood that the development of science policy is very much an iterative process, in which successful and less successful experiences contribute, but political constraints also play an important role. Even successful instruments will lose their value over time. As said by one of the Indian participants, in order to judge the effectiveness of R & D you need a vision of what society is after. Even in such a relatively uncomplicated country as The Netherlands this vision is incomplete, to say the least. In a large, developing and complex society, as in India, a unitary vision is unthinkable.

Part IV: R & D in an international context

In a world divided between the developed countries (where most of the R & D is being carried out) and the developing countries (which have historically lagged behind due to long periods of colonization) what kind of meaningful cooperation in R & D is possible? In the long run, both parties can gain if mutually beneficial programmes are identified under a planned policy framework. Can the principle of equal partnership be recognized in identifying each others' areas of interest? Generation of new knowledge and sharing it with your partner through joint R & D programmes is possible, but the partners may have to respect each other's developmental goals and come to an understanding on the economic implications of such cooperative programmes. Would the short-term economic goals of one partner result in the exploitation of the other? Can there be a more rational division of labour planned through cooperative agreements? Global peace is equally vital for cooperation in science and technology. Regional cooperation in S & T has possibilities of success in Europe and Asia. Are international organizations playing a positive role in promoting S & T cooperation between developing and developed countries? Or will bilateral arrangements be more successful?

Against the background of such questions the chapters highlight several aspects of international scientific cooperation. Professor Rais Ahmed emphasizes the uneven distribution of the world's scientific effort and the asymmetric effects this has on its relevance for the countries' societies, the international movement of scientific manpower and the research opportunities in the diverse countries. While noting that the solution to this problem apparently has to be found by the developing countries themselves, he indicates three areas for fruitful international cooperation: a frank and free discussion of these issues, pure science and networks for data sharing, information bases. Professor J. George Waardenburg's paper has a more theoretical approach: it sketches elements of an economics-inspired theory of research processes, research results and research cooperation as a framework for analysis of the potentialities of cooperation and of the barriers to exploiting them, with practical conclusions similar to the earlier chapter. Dr P.J. Lavakare's chapter points out several global aspects of science policy and emphasizes the need for developing a country-specific science and technology policy, the vexing global context of security and peace issues and the necessity of 'using atoms for peace and not for destruction', the importance of social and human aspects of science and technology. He concludes by quoting the late Mrs Indira Gandhi in her advice to benefit from foreign scientific experience, but 'not to be imprisoned by foreign points of view'. Finally, Professor C. Cooper was asked to put on paper his comments on Waardenburg's chapter, the main argument of which he succinctly summarizes in order to extend it towards a fuller discussion of the increasing constraints to international cooperation on the basis of a free exchange of knowledge as a result of increased commercialization of knowledge.

9 The international dimensions of Indian R & D and international cooperation

Rais Ahmed

The Indo–Dutch debate on science policy issues came at a time when the eighth five-year plan for socio-economic development of India was being evolved, and a certain amount of critical reflection is noticeable in the scientific community. Even though a way out of the Indian dilemmas will have to be found through national efforts, the experience and cooperation of other countries like The Netherlands can play an important role in this process.

PERCEPTION OF S & T AS A TOOL OF ECONOMIC, SOCIAL AND CULTURAL PROGRESS

The importance of science and technology in national reconstruction, thereby creating the possibility of developing a society in India in which the entire population benefits from production and distribution of goods and services, has been recognized since Indian independence in 1947. To use the words of the Scientific Policy Resolution of the government of India passed in March 1958:

The key to National prosperity, apart from the spirit of the people, lies, in the modern age, in the effective combination of three factors, technology, raw-materials and capital, of which the first is perhaps the most important . . . But technology can only grow out of the study of science and its applications . . . It's only through scientific knowledge that reasonable material and cultural amenities and services can be provided for every member of the community, and it is out of a recognition of this possibility that the idea of a welfare state has grown.

Along with this utilitarian and socio-economic aspect of science, there was a clear recognition of the cultural aspect in the following words:

Science has led to the growth and diffusion of culture to an extent never possible before. It has not only radically altered man's material environment, but, what is of still deeper significance, it has provided new tools of thought and has extended man's mental horizon. It has thus influenced even the basic values of life, and given to civilization a new vitality and a new dynamism.

NECESSITY FOR ECONOMIC PLANNING

It may be recalled that at the end of the colonial period India had a literacy rate of about 10 per cent, and in the cases of women, rural areas and other sizeable groups of population, the percentage was much lower. There was abject poverty, a great dearth of doctors and medical assistance and no electricity or drinking water in hundreds and thousands of homes. It was obvious that in the face of such acute human suffering, it would be the first duty of a government — which had been installed following a century of struggle by these same poor but determined people — to provide quick remedies to the situation. It would not have sufficed to depend entirely on market operations investment, which would have gone in the directions that would bring in the maximum of profits and was not concerned with remedying a particular situation. New industries had to be created including heavy and machine-tool industries; and much needed goods had to be produced; food production had to be augmented; services had to be established with inputs of education, training and research. Even if such industry or production was not internationally competitive, it had to be protected in the nascent stage so as to take root and grow. This was the basic need of the country; without fulfilling it neither the misery of the people could be alleviated nor the nation consolidated. Planning for economic development thus became a necessity and it was taken up with the greatest speed and care. Recognizing the constructive role of science from its inception the Planning Commission has always included a scientist.

EXPANSION OF S & T ENTERPRISE

In pursuance of a policy to achieve these ends, the country has made great advances in all spheres. Education has expanded manifold and we have today more than half a million schools, more than 5,000 colleges of all kinds and 150 universities. Scientific research was done in India on a small scale even in the pre-independence period, when scientists worked under very adverse circumstances but had upheld the great tradition of science from ancient through medieval and modern times. Today the base of scientific and technological research in India is fairly massive. Research is done in hundreds of educational institutions, covering practically all areas of science, with an enrolment of around 20,000 scholars in these institutions, and a production of around 4,000 PhDs every year. Research, particularly of an applied kind, has basically grown in hundreds of laboratories or research stations which have been set up for the purpose under various departments of government (See Part V Chapter 13). The National Policy of Education which was approved by Parliament in 1986, in its Programme of Action, has a major chapter on research and development, where great stress has been laid on linkage among the centres of research in the universities and outside, and between all these centres and industry, agriculture and services. Our known weakness is in the inadequacy of these linkages.

INTERNATIONAL COOPERATION AND SUPPORT

Of course, this network is intimately connected with scientists and institutions abroad. Government departments and other agencies have numerous agreements with other countries in specified fields of work, such as the agreement we have with The Netherlands since March 1986 in instrumentation, astronomy and other areas. Taking advantage of the fact that India has followed a policy of non-alignment which has been based on rejecting the idea of tutelage of any power, ordinary or super; and of objective consideration of issues, it has had deep and expanding relations with the Soviet Union and the United States of America. At the moment there are seventy joint projects under Indo–Soviet science and technology cooperation, involving research laboratories and universities covering many fields of science from astrophysics to hydrology, laser fusion to high-temperature superconductors, from biotechnology to nuclear reactors. On the other hand, Indo–American cooperation is equally, if not more, prominent. There are more than 300 Indo–American collaborative science and technology projects aided by a dozen American technical agencies, involving an exchange of nearly 1,000 leading scientists annually. All this is in addition to the free movement of students and scholars to all parts of the world because the Indian society is an open democratic society.

REFLECTION ON THE ACHIEVEMENT OF GOALS

When one reflects on all this enterprise and international connections and tries to see how far the social purposes which science and technology were expected to serve have actually been served, one feels perturbed. The objective truth seems to be that progress has been great, but it has not been as much as expected. More than this, the quality of the progress leaves much to be desired. There are still great disparities in the way our people live and there is great poverty and backwardness. Education is perhaps an indicator, and here in spite of the seemingly massive advance in enrolment and the number of institutions, the literacy rate is still less than 40 per cent and the number of illiterates has actually increased in the period of independence because of the increase in population. It is a matter of concern as to what will be the time span required for full literacy, and the concomitant improvement in conditions of living and assuring nutrition, health, shelter and clothing to our people. Perhaps, even scientists now realize that science and technology cannot solve social and economic problems unless they are utilized by society within a framework of its social, economic and political policies. It is a matter of greater concern that many of the impediments seem to be almost insurmountable because they are attributable to the very nature of science in the present times, and to the dissemination of scientific knowledge in the world.

RESTRICTIONS IN THE FREE FLOW AND UTILIZATION OF KNOWLEDGE

When India started with the idea of reconstructing its society with the help of science and technology, it perhaps innocently believed that the scientific world was one, and science was universal, that there was a free flow of scientific knowledge. If much of it was in the West, it was still something like a bank of knowledge from which one could draw according to one's need. It was soon realized, however, that the reality was quite different, and that science, as well as technology, was riddled with restrictions, and the restrictions were related to the very fact that science has great applications in practical life, in industry, in defence and in the making of profits. Trade secrets have existed for a long time, but in recent decades one is now faced with 'restricted' and 'classified' categories of knowledge. Today, technology is the basis of success in trade, and of economic advantage, and ultimately of the domination of those who have it over those who don't have it. Researchers know that neither materials nor ideas are freely available; if special materials are needed for space research or for fabrication of electronic devices, the market is as good as closed. Much of technology is proprietary, and the prices which have to be paid to get it ensure that the goods that will be produced with that technology will not be internationally competitive. The cold war and the armaments race have made the situation worse because anything can be said to have 'dual purpose' and, therefore, its supply, be it a computer or a machine tool, can be cut off. What is worse, is that there is a monopoly in this field. If one great country says that something cannot be given to India, none of the other developed countries in the free world can dare to do otherwise.

It is well known that the transfer of scientific knowledge through formal sources like publication of journals is only a minor contribution. Most of the scientific inter-connection and transfer of knowledge takes place through person-to-person contact in conferences, by telephone or through correspondence. Therefore, countries in the underdeveloped world, with shortages of foreign exchange and with global distances to travel, are put to a great disadvantage, even if the restrictions were not there. Our quest for being up-to-date and our striving for excellence are given big set-backs by this situation.

CONSEQUENCES OF UNDERDEVELOPMENT

In fact, our chances of doing good research are seriously limited by the allocations we are able to make for R & D. It is known that all the developing countries put together do not spend even 2–3 per cent of what is spent on scientific and technological research in the developed countries of the West (leaving aside the socialist countries). Therefore, with the little money which India can afford, even though it is 1 per cent of its GNP, it has to depend on the scientific knowledge coming through the journals. This represents something which is two to three years out of date, and which does not always represent the front line of scientific work. It is again well known that the great scientific advances in the

West are in fields of endeavour which may have limited relevance for India. For example, in fields such as defence, space orientated research, automation and synthetic materials. Yet, because it is prestigious to do 'front-line' research, many of the scientists and scientific institutions in India are carried away by the glamour of these less relevant areas, and spend great time and effort on tackling problems arising out of these fields, rather than solving problems related to society and the national economy. Naturally, there is a misallocation of resources or, at least, less than optimal allocation of resources. Just to take one example, India is faced with an expenditure of around two billion dollars in developing what is believed will be a suitable aircraft for the airforce, likely to emerge in the mid-1990s. One does not know what the configuration of the world will be in ten to fifteen years, or if there is going to be a sustained international *détente*, which some world leaders are proclaiming.

One must also mention the natural adversity of the less-developed countries in that tens of thousands of professionals seem to be migrating to the developed countries especially to the United States. Nearly 40,000 professionals enter the United States every year from other countries of the world, and India contributes a sizeable number of these. There are prestigious institutes of technology in India but a good proportion of their output migrates and even settles down in the United States. As excellent postgraduates are produced and research training is provided in any of the currently front-line fields such as biotechnology or computer science or superconductivity, these people become instantly available for international hiring. Here again, the advanced level of research and the challenges and opportunities available for first-rate scientific work provide a natural attraction to young people; but with such massive leakages of highly competent professionals, trained at great cost, how are the developing countries to create a human resource and a base for scientific and technological work?

One must mention another interesting feature of great relevance. Recently the geosynchronous Indian Satellite INSAT-1C was launched by Europe's *Ariane* space launch vehicle. The chairman of the European agency disclosed that India paid 47 million dollars for the launch; furthermore India is going to pay 70 million dollars for each of the INSAT launches in 1990 and 1991. The chairman also mentioned that the eight-year-old European agency was floated by some eleven European consortia and its present worth is 2 billion dollars. If India were to develop its own launch capacity, the heavy commitments of expenditure could hardly be justified, unless the intention would be to enter the commercial business of launching space satellites. The same applies to many other fields, particularly aircraft and other military hardware. It is just not possible for developing countries to compete in many fields of technology. The point is also valid, to some extent, for the scientific work of excellent quality which is being done in the field of high-temperature superconductivity. Even if one succeeds in the scientific work, world-wide technological exploitation will probably still be done by the developed countries.

LACK OF INTERNATIONAL SUPPORT FOR REMEDIAL ACTION

The above-mentioned factors tend to counter every effort to overcome underdevelopment and in fact perpetuate it because on the one hand it is related to such basic characteristics of science as its applicability to economic development and human welfare, its international comparability and even sheer excellence. On the other hand the developed countries have consistently refused to recognize that the problem exists, let alone saying anything about doing something to overcome it. Individual scientists are very sympathetic, and institutions are willing to help, but the system is larger than all of them put together and the system is not an entity which can have sympathy. It is merciless. The United Nations Conference on Science, Technology and Development (Vienna 1979) was a forum which clearly revealed that the developed countries were not even prepared to support the notion that the developing countries must make an extraordinary effort to develop their own independent science and technology, reducing dependence on the developed countries, or that their share in world R & D should be raised in the next ten to fifteen years, from 2 or 3 per cent to 20 per cent. A pitiably small international fund of 50 million dollars had been suggested to provide special assistance to the developing countries, and needless to say, that has remained an idle recommendation.

It is obvious that the developing countries have to find a solution to this problem themselves. The responsibility is not only that of the scientists and technologists in this country, but also of those who make the larger socio-economic policy. A different basic approach to solving the problems of human suffering and backwardness will have to be evolved and scientific and technological problems arising from such an endeavour will have to be the first target of work. The problems will not be at the nut and bolt level; they will be found to be related to deeper problems in each field of science and they will need the most advanced ideas and technologies. But what can the well-meaning international community of scientists and of institutions do to help in this direction? That is a question which one should briefly answer.

SUGGESTIONS REGARDING COOPERATIVE ACTION

The first obvious step seems to be that the world community of scientists should itself clearly understand the kind of crisis in scientific endeavour and its application to human welfare which the developing countries face. The understanding of the issues can be improved by a frank and free discussion between the developed and the developing countries — even if the idea of a well-to-do India being a great market for goods from, say, The Netherlands, contributing to the health of the world economy, is not particularly appealing. Even if the world consequences of under development leading to great problems of resource depletion and environmental hazards is a matter of indifference, the dormant intellectual resource of 800 million people of India contributing ideas and inventions to world science should be attractive. A determined effort to analyse deeply and sympathetically perceive the problems of a developing country like India will help ultimately to change the international climate, which includes a change towards a free flow of scientific and technological knowledge. The United Nations, Unesco, the Non-Aligned Movement, and the Pugwash Movement are already exerting pressure of this kind, but a wider base of scientific opinion is needed. The Indo–Dutch joint debate should certainly 'set the ball rolling'.

The second area of cooperation is in the various fields of pure science. In this sphere perhaps the flow of knowledge is less hindered than elsewhere, and therefore, exchange of scientists between countries to work in each others' laboratories and universities, working on joint projects, is easier to plan and the returns from such cooperation could be very exciting. There should be an understanding that all the basic materials for undertaking desired research will be procured by common effort. The less clearly understood process of pure research priming applied research is bound to come into operation in its own time, and hence at least the capability to solve problems of a national character would be improved. Therefore, cooperation in pure scientific research and education must be encouraged.

Third, perhaps everyone will agree that linkages, coordination and general organization of national research all suffer because the data and information base is very deficient. In the belief that The Netherlands is better off in this field, it is suggested that cooperation will be very fruitful in this area. One may venture the opinion that the Indian policy and hence planning have also been eclectic and even *ad hoc*. A tradition of scholarly studies, including procedures of review and evaluation, sectoral or otherwise, has to be built in future. The S & T or R & D activities should be linked more effectively with common social and economic interests. Technology assessment as well as technology forecast are going to be emerging activities in future. The S & T development prospects have to be combined with market expectations of the two partners. The European experience could give Indian activities a fillip if training of personnel through work experience could be established in these critical areas of creating an information base, the undertaking of impact and performance studies, and technology evaluation and forecast.

10 International R & D cooperation in a North–South perspective: some theoretical and practical issues

J. George Waardenburg

INTRODUCTION

This chapter, though finally aiming at some practical insight into the international dimension of R & D and international scientific cooperation, begins by taking a theoretical approach in the belief that 'nothing is as practical as a good theory'. Unfortunately, such a theory is not readily available. Therefore the chapter restricts itself to putting up some building blocks for such a theory at the microlevel of research processes, which could contribute to working out a theoretical framework, but may be sufficient in this form for throwing some light on several aspects of international scientific cooperation. The opening section sketches a stylized scheme of six steps in a research process while the next section lists some facts which play a role in the production of scientific knowledge in the way economists discuss production factors. However, special emphasis is given to the so-called 'public good' character of some of these factors and of the product, that is that their use by one factor does not exclude the use by other factors of the same good. Some of the possible implications of these theoretical notions for international cooperation are then discussed, while in the concluding section the impact of the realities of international relations on North–South scientific cooperation are considered.

STAGES IN THE RESEARCH PROCESS

For reference, even if it is not always used explicitly, we shall sketch briefly the model of stages of the research process which the author has in the back of his mind when discoursing further on factors in research and international cooperation. Figure 10.1 gives an ideal scheme of research processes in six stages, A–F, connected by five phases (1)–(5). In principle it is thought that the scheme may apply to research processes in different disciplines, that is not only in the sciences but also in the humanities and social sciences, and some distinctions of the scheme may even have validity for development in the R & D sense, but no attempt is made to spell out the latter. Also no distinction is made between pure or basic and applied research nor between these kinds and the in-between kind of use-directed basic research in order not to complicate things unnecessarily.

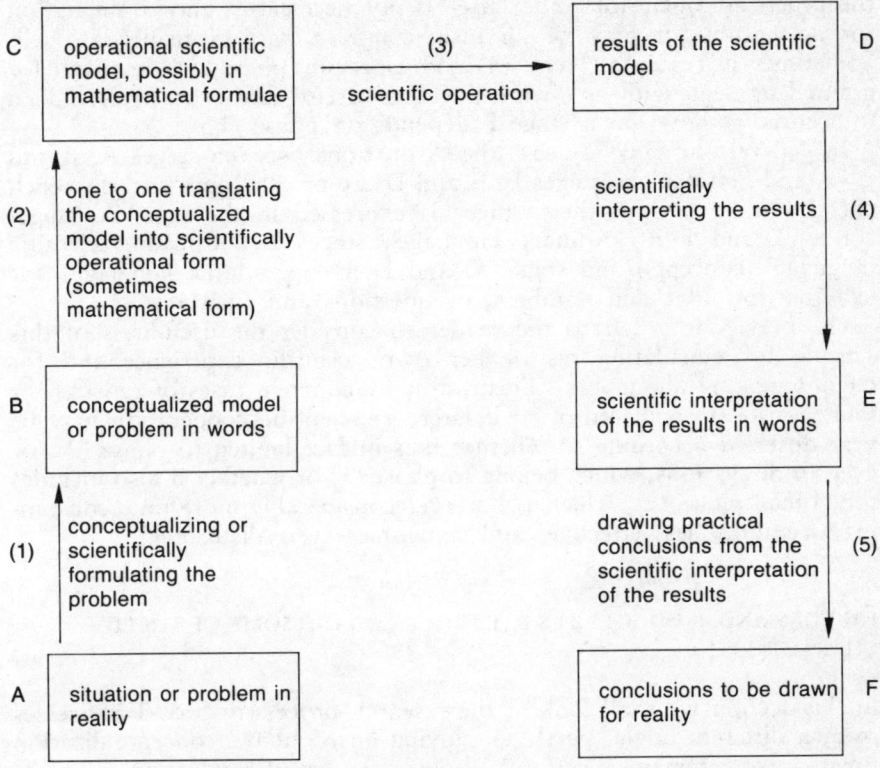

*Figure 10.1   Schematic representation of five phases of a research process
(1)–(5), and the six stages, A–F, connected by the phases*

The main object of distinguishing the stages and phases is to emphasize
the distinction between stage B, the conceptual mode, and stage C, the
operational model and thereby emphasizing the difference between phase
(1), conceptualizing the situation or problem in reality, and phase (2),
translating this conceptual model into operational form. While phase (1)
is normally decisive and fundamental — as the real assumptions and
limitations of scientific research are made in this phase — phase (2) is
more technical. In practice a lot of research actually starts from stage B
or even from stage C, accepting some standard formulations for those
stages of earlier research and not repeating the fundamental analysis at
their level but sometimes making small variations in the standard
formulations. Examples of operational models, stage C, are mathematical
models, experimental designs, questionnaires in the social sciences, etc.
Often phase (3), the scientific operation, is seen as the heart of scientific
activity (calculations, experiments, data collecting) with phase (4) or
stage E, the scientific interpretation, as the keystone, but often the results
at stage E are already largely determined or at least circumscribed by the
crucial conceptionalizations of phase (1).

Another distinction which is revealed in this scheme is that between
phase (4) and phase (5), that between the 'scientific interpretation' and

the practical conclusion. The latter is not necessarily only a suggestion for action, but it may be an insight into a part of reality as well. Sometimes in research, phase (4) and especially phase (5) are taken for granted or dealt with as obvious, with a careful further analysis and an indication of how much stage F depends on phase (1).

In general one may say that the distinctions between stages A, B and C on and between the stages F, E and D are parallel ones and that each corresponding pair of these stages is expressed in the same language: stages A and F in 'ordinary language', stages B and E in 'scientific language' (concepts) and stages C and D in 'operational language' (for example formulae and numbers, or questions and answers).

For brevity it is left to the reader to consider the usefulness of this scheme for elucidating his or her own scientific experience and for communicating about it, to illustrate it by concrete cases of research or to reject it. We will return to it later, as scientific cooperation may be very different according to whether it is in fact limited to phase (3), or even to discussions, which belong to phase (5) or whether it also includes the crucial phase (2), which is however considerably more time consuming, seemingly less effective, and sometimes even 'disturbing'.

FACTORS AND PRODUCTS IN S & T PROCESSES AND SOME OF THEIR CHARACTERISTICS

In this section we shall look at the research process or S & T processes from a different angle, partly employing an economic conceptualization for it — in as far as we can talk about a process of production of 'scientific knowledge' as output — in which factors of 'scientific production' are used as inputs. In fact we shall take a micro approach by talking about separate research processes, while economists referring to research and technical change have usually taken a more macro point of view (Arrow, 1962a).[1] The dynamic character of these research processes will be mentioned. Next, we will use the concept of a 'public good' to characterize some of the factors and the product of research processes. Then we will indicate different kinds or levels of research which have a certain hierarchical order, but also a certain interdependency. Finally, locational aspects are discussed.

One way of looking at S & T is to see it as a more or less continuous production process, which nevertheless can be conceptualized usefully as a succession of research projects in order to bring out the inner dynamics of the process. For simplicity's sake these research projects can be thought of as having the same duration or as taking place during successive time periods of the same length, while in each period many projects may take place simultaneously.

Each of these projects can be conceived of as a production process with several factors of production, the combined application of which gives a certain output, scientific insight.[2]

As factors which contribute to this production process we can mention the following:

a. the *stock of scientific knowledge* created before and available at the beginning of the project;
b. the *degree of relevance* of this scientific knowledge for the project's research;
c. the *conceptual skills* (skilled manpower), comprising both a command of the relevant scientific knowledge and the ability to conceptionalize the problem to be dealt with adequately;
d. the *technical skills* (skilled manpower) devoted to the project;
e. the *capital goods* (such as instruments) used in the project;
f. the *research climate* in which the project is carried out.

Some of the factors mentioned may sound very familiar to those at home in economic jargon, others require some elucidation. The first factor mentioned, the stock of scientific knowledge, is of the same nature as the output of the project. It differs from the latter, however, in its timing, as it has to become available one or more periods before the project's output, which in itself may be an input to research projects in later time periods. Because of this difference in time the present conceptualization of a research process is essentially dynamic.

Moreover, this general 'stock of knowledge' is much less specific than the project's result. The second factor, the degree of relevance of the first factor, is supposed to define the more specific aspect of scientific knowledge which is relevant to the project. We shall refrain from having a discussion on the nature of knowledge, and on defining its degree of relevance for the project.

While (skilled) manpower is well known as a factor of production in economics, the distinction between conceptual skills and technical skills goes back to the scheme in Figure 10.1. Conceptual skills are those specifically used in phase (1) of conceptualization, and partly also in phase (2), but the technical skills are primarily useful in phase (3), the scientific operation, and only partly in phase (2).

While capital goods are familiar to economists, the idea of a research climate as distinct from the stock of scientific knowledge may look very strange. This stock of scientific knowledge resembles the level of technology and its representation in the economic theory of production and growth as proposed in its early stage by Tinbergen (1942) and Solow (1957).

This admittedly vague concept stands both for a certain 'scientific culture', a combination of understanding research as a particular approach to reality, of an accumulated experience with doing research[3] and of a value and possibly incentive system which guides researchers in their concrete research behaviour in a more general way than their particular skills do. This concept is possibly useful if we make a spatial distinction between different places of research. Moreover, this concept brings another dynamic element into the conceptualization of the research process as the research climate may develop over time, possibly under the influence of the research activities and cooperation discussed in this chapter.[4]

It may be clear that we cannot go into a discussion of the degree of measurability of the factors or of the output mentioned above. The general idea is that the output would be positively related to each of the factors mentioned, however measured.

As a next step in trying to outline some characteristics of the research process, which might usefully be taken into account in a discussion of international S & T cooperation, we introduce the notion of a 'public good', which was rediscovered by the American economist Samuelson[5] after a much earlier exposition of it by the Swedish economist Wicksell. A public good, as distinguished from private goods which are dealt with in most of the economic literature, has the interesting characteristic that use or enjoyment of the good by somebody does not prevent or hinder somebody else from using or enjoying the same good at the same time. Sometimes the difficulty of excluding or preventing somebody from using the good is mentioned as an additional characteristic. We will call this the 'inappropriability' of the public good. Well known examples are broadcasts, national defence and lighthouses. There are also partial public goods, for example the beauty of landscape or roads, which can be spoiled by overcrowding. The important of public goods in economics is that, in contradistinction to private goods for which in many cases normal markets can coordinate their production and consumption very competently, it is very difficult to think of market arrangements which would provide people with the proper amounts of these public goods. This suggests that non-market ways of collective decisionmaking are appropriate to this end.

Scientific knowledge or research results are examples *par excellence* of public goods: enjoying their insights, building further on them or using them for applications does not prevent others from doing the same at the same time.

This becomes more evident if one contrasts this situation with material products, which are an application of research — or rather R & D — results. In general they will not have the public good character of the research results, and they will be very suitable for marketing and providing the basis for securing a profit in the market. This is exactly why industries making such products engage in R & D, in order to be able to reap the benefit of its application via these products. As however the products often reveal the research behind them, other producers may soon compete against them with the same or similar applications of their research, against which there is no natural protection. As this would discourage the enterprises from engaging in R & D, the patent system has been developed in order to protect the inventors for some time against such competition, thus removing to a large extent the disincentive mentioned.[6]

Interestingly, within the S & T system one finds considerable parts of it carried out under the inducement, financial or otherwise, of non-market bodies like governments. In the past kings, but also organizations like academies, performed such non-market roles. In such situations, where material benefits are difficult to connect with research achievements, one sometimes finds complex non-material incentive systems related to prestige, reputation, status and research opportunities.

Incidentally, not only research results have this public good character, but also the 'research climate' may be conceived of as a local, public good. Even the availability of conceptual skills in a certain project may come near to being a public good in as far as the use of the conceptional skill may have a peculiar time structure and require relatively little time.

While the use of a public good may not prevent its use by other actors, its acquisition may require certain efforts or costs. This is to a certain extent the case for local public goods like landscapes or lighthouses, which can only be used at the 'cost' of moving to the appropriate locality. But the access to research results in themselves may require a considerable effort of study and the acquisition of publications. In fact the whole gamut of scientific publication and information activities is witness of such costs, though they need not be paid for by the users themselves. The 'grey literature' may be cheaper, but is usually limited to an 'in' group of users. These costs and limitations of access to scientific knowledge may also be strangely localized in the sense that they are (relatively) absent in certain places and high elsewhere. Research 'climate' may be an example of such a locally freely available good. Sometimes even the research instrumentation can be near to such a locally freely available good, as long as no serious crowding of its use occurs.

Before turning our attention to the implications of these still largely theoretical notions for international research cooperation we want to draw attention to one more features of S & T research. It displays a certain hierarchical structure, indicated in Figure 10.2, of layers of qualitatively different research activities, where the activities composed of higher-numbered layers comprise more or less those of a lower-numbered layer or even build on them, giving a certain direction and perspective to the latter in their turn.

The difference between these layers is often determined not so much in the technical quality of phase 3 but in the quality of phase 1, and in a way also of phase 2 of a research project as indicated in Figure 10.1

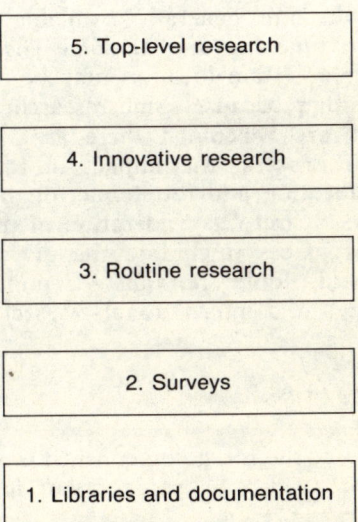

Figure 10.2 Layers of research

and earlier in this chapter; it may also have something to do with a 'research climate'. This explains why researchers who have participated in research of the type in layers 4 or 5 at a given place are often able to introduce such research elsewhere if they move, something more than 'technical skills' and training in them being at stake here. This is one of the advantages of (inter)national research cooperation, even if it is implemented only temporarily, as this quality or conceptual aspect of the research process is carried over in cooperation more easily than technical skills. By saying this I by no means intend to degrade the importance of technical skills, but it appears that something more than those alone, together with research facilities, play a role in the quality of research.

It would take too long here to spell out other implications of the distinction of these layers and their interdependence for international cooperation which may become somewhat specific in certain situations, but from experience with research such implications can be further deduced.

Location can play an important role in research. Often certain places acquire a good 'name' in certain research areas; is this a matter of confusing good researchers with the location where they work? Is it wrong to think about stimulating (inter)national research cooperation not only by connecting individual researchers with each other but also by connecting places of research?

It appears that in describing a place of research more is required than simply listing the skills of the individual researchers and the available research facilities.[7] The degree of cooperation, openness, exchange of ideas and general management are also important, but especially the presence of a research tradition and research climate, including the relatively free availability of conceptual skills. Moreover, the ready access to earlier research results reached at a location make their input in further research easier and 'cheaper'.[8]

While research results are generally available outside a location, perhaps with a certain time lag and at some cost, also some aspects relating to the work at a certain location may be available to a limited degree to 'outsiders', either because some researchers leave the location temporarily, or others are welcomed there as guests. The locational aspect of the research process, the impact of location on choice of subjects and conceptualization and the impact of these in turn on international research make a careful consideration of the question of where research actually takes places (including the distinction between First World and Third World), quite relevant for understanding the international research process and international research cooperation.

INTERNATIONAL COOPERATION

Against the background of the foregoing considerations some general and largely theoretical remarks can be made about international scientific cooperation.

First of all, scientific research is international by nature. Not only is its product, research results, a public good, but it can be shared by publications all over the world at relatively little cost, and it is therefore a good example of a global public good.

This holds also for its main ingredient, research results in former periods. And in fact one sees a world wide network of publications (formal ones like books and journals as well as informal or grey ones such as 'preliminary' research reports and the accompanying scientific correspondence) which are an important form of international scientific cooperation, even if partly on a commercial basis and organized as a market.

However, the research processes themselves are by no means public, whatever that would mean anyhow, and they are strongly localized. They take place at a certain location, within a certain laboratory with certain equipment and within a limited group of researchers. This has important consequences.

Researchers or research groups can technically quite easily prevent global publication of their research results, and either keep the results for some time completely secret or known to only a small 'in' group. This could be done in order to be able to claim the research results only once a definite or advanced stage has been reached, or in order to transform the results first into economic goods. In fact a considerable part of global research is kept confidential, mainly for military or commercial reasons.

Furthermore, research itself is a learning process not only in the sense that further research can build on earlier research but also in the sense that experienced researchers develop only over periods of many years, even given a strong research inclination and the rare natural gifts which they need to possess anyway. This is an additional reason why true scientists are scarce, and why the costs spent on their education by society are increasingly recovered over their lifetime. 'Brain drain' therefore becomes a profitable business, and an added cost to the country of origin.

Another consequence of the localized nature of research processes is that two equally skilled researchers may have to work in totally different research situations, in terms of facilities and other stimuli, and therefore may work with very different effectiveness. The reputation they may acquire in this way also affects their future research opportunities.

All in all it would be naïve to conclude from the international and public-good character of research that international cooperation will arise automatically to an optimum extent. There are many serious barriers in practice and in trying to bring down some of them one can be comforted by the notion that one is fighting against man- or society-made barriers, but that one is doing so in accordance with the nature of research, and not against the personal or scientific interests of the researchers.

This brings us to the consideration of some practical and constructive aspects of international cooperation. We mentioned above that the international network of written research communications is already one — partly commercialized — obvious form of international scientific contact and cooperation. It may not be functioning optimally, but is difficult to improve this global network bilaterally.

The international cooperation which is the subject of this chapter concerns, however, more forms of cooperation than perfecting the system of research publications, however important that is. We will give special attention to the matter of bringing researchers into direct contact with each other.

It may be useful to distinguish at least five different forms of such cooperation:

A. Brief visits of some weeks by one or more researchers to another country in order to give some lectures or to get acquainted with some researchers and research centres in the other country.
B. Workshops in which recent research results and experiences can be exchanged and discussed.
C. Research stays of longer periods (from a few months to one or two years) in which the visiting researcher either has his own life of individual research (juxtaposition) or takes part in the ongoing research (participation).
D. Research stays of longer periods in which a cooperatively designed and joint research plan is carried out (complete cooperation).
E. Special-purpose visits, mostly of an instructional kind.

Of these activities complete cooperation is by far the most complex and difficult one, and not always necessary for a good cooperative programme.

A mixture of several kinds of activities is often seen to be most efficient; only 'A' activities constitute no cooperative research programme, and 'A + B' activities hardly one.

These activities should be clearly distinguished from two kinds of supportive activities in cooperative programmes:

a. Planning and designing activities
b. Administrative implementation-supporting activities

They are necessary components of a programme, but do not constitute it.

What are the possible advantages or benefits and disadvantages or costs of such personal cooperation in the light of the points made earlier? First we shall look at some possible disadvantages or costs.

If international (research) cooperation were a different activity than research itself, it would carry the same type of costs as research itself, viz., primarily the time of researchers involved and possibly the use of equipment which would have to be withdrawn from the normal research activities. However, this is hardly the case as international cooperation is in principle simply continuing the research one is doing, only in a special, cooperative way.

Only some researchers have to move to other places and adapt to the circumstances there, which may sometimes by easy, sometimes quite cumbersome both materially and psychologically and normally the greater the difference between the researchers' usual circumstances and their new environment the harder it will be. The interest in international cooperation on the part of the researchers involved in it is an important and often decisive factor for its success, and as researchers are, in the final analysis, most interested in doing research, it is important that these accommodation costs are minimized by the creation of a good material and personal infrastructure which will not damage the researchers or the research. Often these costs are overlooked or underestimated, thus creating a disincentive for the researchers. Travel and extra board and lodging costs are only one aspect of these costs, but they have to be provided adequately and often comprise the main visible, because budgetary, cost of cooperation.

A second disadvantage of 'cost' could be the necessity for some of the researchers to adjust their line of research somewhat, as a part of the cooperative effort. In some cases this might be an advantageous adjustment, but for the cases where this is not clearly so it could be useful to consider that in principle only 'complete cooperation' as indicated above involves such costs, while several simpler forms of cooperation create most of the benefits which we now shall consider.

The advantages or benefits of international cooperation are quite different in different disciplines. Often in the humanities and the social sciences (including economics) phenomena are studied which are specific for certain countries, areas or locations. If researchers from outside these countries, etc. want to study such phenomena, there is a specific advantage to be gained from collaboration with researchers within the countries concerned.[9] And in some of the natural sciences, such as geology and biology, certain research objects are location specific. This advantage of international cooperation will not be discussed further, however, as it is absent in most S & T research.

Another advantage exists if very large and expensive instruments are required, which provide research facilities for a large group of researchers, for example in nuclear physics, astronomy or space research. In such cases large and rich countries are in a more advantageous position. For other countries cooperation is obviously desirable from a cost-sharing point of view, if one wants to engage in that particular line of research at all.[10]

Also where there are frequent, rapid technological improvements in scientific equipment which lower cost levels there are likely to be advantages in international cooperation. If equipment is shared, then continual, expensive updating is not needed by anyone who has an interest. Clearly all this concerns the capital factor in research.

But there are other advantages of a less material nature. The most important of these is probably not technical skill but conceptual skill. The researchers from different sides learn from each other the way they conceive the problems to be tackled and the methods they conceive for tackling them. To profit most from such an exchange they should already possess sufficient technical skill to be able to see and implement the practical research consequences of the conceptual stage, but the experience of a common scientific spirit notwithstanding the considerable differences between the researchers and their differing backgrounds can be very stimulating. Such transfers can take place in increasing intensity especially in workshops, institutions of juxtaposition, participation and 'complete cooperation', respectively.

Another benefit to researchers which comes rather automatically from international cooperation is the direct access to each other's research results, but also access to and understanding of other research results that can occur, again in increasing intensity, during short visits — at an admittedly very low level — at workshops and during long exchanges.

Such a conceptualization of international research cooperation may serve several objectives. It may relate a discussion on international scientific cooperation to the nature of research activities itself and may help to identify possible benefits and costs of such cooperation. And finally, it may serve the proper design of a programme of such cooperation.

INTERNATIONAL REALITIES AND NORTH–SOUTH SCIENTIFIC COOPERATION

After the largely theoretical observations in the earlier sections some more pragmatic remarks will be added in this section.[11] They will take into account more explicitly the context for which this chapter is intended, that is international scientific cooperation between developed and developing countries and in particular that between India and The Netherlands.

'Something like 95 to 98 per cent of the world's research and development is carried out in a few developed countries and only 2 to 5 per cent is carried out in the developing countries'.[12] This means that the conceptualization and the choice of problems dealt with in research is largely determined in developed countries. In some disciplines and in fundamental research this may not make much difference but in other disciplines and in strategic and in applied research this factor may be quite relevant.[13] Moreover, the 'learning by doing' process takes place in developed countries, and in order to make developing countries' researchers also profit from it, international cooperation is essential.

A not inconsiderable part of all research is of a military nature and is kept secret.[14] Its applications in the form of new weaponry are also kept secret for some time. This limits the total area of scientific endeavour open for international cooperation. Another large part of all research is done in private by multinational companies and often is also withheld from outsiders, sometimes even long before commercial applications have been developed and can be patented. The need for secrecy and patenting certainly increases private companies' expenditures on R & D, but do not enlarge the area for international scientific cooperation.

Such situations unfortunately put limits on international scientific cooperation, which, in the former subsection, was shown as a relatively cheap means to somewhat counterbalance the highly uneven North–South research distribution. Even worse, these factors also limit the normal access to research results via publication, making it more difficult for researchers in the Third World to catch up with their colleagues in the First World who have more personal contacts with researchers engaged in shielded research.

Researchers ought to minimize these limitations as far as compatible with reasonable demands by their military or private company authorities. With some sensible thought and imagination in research organization, many opportunities could be better utilized in this context.

Although some of the odds against which the LDCs are placed when they try to reap the benefits of research have already been spelled out, two other facts should be mentioned which aggravate this situation. One well-known fact is the braindrain from LDCs to DCs because of the greater wealth and research opportunities in the latter countries. Another, less-known, fact is that a result of a study on European scientific cooperation showed that 'the more basic the research topic on which collaboration is taking place, the greater the probability of successful collaboration' and 'the stronger the national capability in research in the field that was being undertaken collaboratively the greater the success from the point of view of that particular country'.[15] This suggests that the choice of subjects and participants in international collaboration should be carefully made in order that the collaboration does not give rise to an even greater disparity of benefits.[16]

Another interesting research result, this time from the area of 'science dynamics' or 'sociology of the sciences', is that attempts to steer the development of research areas by non-scientists are generally totally unsuccessful: scientific developments are nearly always determined by forces from within the scientific community.

Such a result is relevant for the design of international cooperation programmes in as much as it is wise also to follow forces and motivations operating within the research world itself. In general it is important to organize a programme in such a way that as soon as possible the initiative is put in the hands of the researchers concerned, and to let them make mutual arrangements, within agreed boundaries, regarding the design and procedures of the programme.

Oldham (1980) makes a useful distinction between North–South cooperation in basic research and 'in scientific research which has developmental objectives'. It appears useful to have both types of research contributions in a programme, provided two conditions are satisfied. One is that the 'North' researchers acknowledge the final responsibility and expertise of the 'South' researchers to make judgements about the usefulness of the research with regard to developmental objectives. The other is that one type of research is not played off against the other type, but that especially on the part of the designers of the programme (in particular in the case of India with a very complex developing society) the complementarity of basic research and developmental research is recognized.

Udgaonkar (1980, p. 111), quoting from the Scientific Policy Resolution, rightly emphasizes this point: 'it is an inherent obligation of a great country like India, with its tradition of scholarship and original thinking and great cultural heritage, to participate fully in the march of science, which is probably mankind's greatest enterprise today. What is also often forgotten is that a mind trained in 'useless' but challenging areas like high-energy physics or cosmic rays may also contribute in other very useful areas when the need and opportunity arise'. In general one may say that in developing countries building up an indigenous capacity for research for the future is more important than quickly to acquire research results from elsewhere.

These and other issues related to science and technology and to North–South cooperation in this field have been dealt with extensively at the United Nations Conference on Science and Technology for Development

(UNCSTED) in Vienna, 1979. For this conference the 'Pugwash Guidelines for International Scientific Cooperation for Development' were a useful framework as a 'code of conduct'. They are still relevant and could also be usefully employed in bilateral S & T cooperation programmes.

It may be noted that in 1987 the Dutch government, and in particular the ministry of education and science, has initiated a new policy which emphasizes the importance of internationalization of education and research in The Netherlands. A result of this policy was the support for participation in cooperative programmes like the one between India and The Netherlands in Science and Technology which was mentioned explicitly in the related documents.

Four collaborative programmes between India and The Netherlands are in existence now.

a. In the social sciences: the Indo–Dutch Programme on Alternatives in Development (IDPAD), administered by the Indian Council of Social Science Research (ICSSR) in new Delhi, and the Institute for Societal Research in Developing Countries (IMWOO) at the Hague.
b. In agrarian research: a programme administered by both ministries of agriculture.
c. In S & T research: a programme administered by the department of science and technology at New Delhi and the department of science policy of the ministry of education and sciences, Netherlands University Foundation for International Cooperation at Zoetermeer, the Hague.
d. Programme of 'scientific research and technical higher education', administered by the ministry of human resources at New Delhi and the department of higher education of the ministry of education and sciences at Zoetermeer.

Such programmes may be enhanced not only by choosing the proper areas for cooperation in research but also by occasional discussions among participants of the dimensions of the research endeavour and opportunities for international scientific cooperation.

NOTES

1. Professor Charles Cooper has drawn my attention to this paper by Arrow, who also contributed other papers and valuable insights (Arrow 1962b, 1965, 1969). See also Nelson (1959). A more micro approach, but then directed mostly at the development of R & D is to be found in: Marschak *et al.* (1967).
2. In the discussion of this paper, again Professor Charles Cooper has drawn attention to the essentially stochastic nature of such a production process, given the uncertainty of results inherent to the nature of research. While this observation is correct, for simplicity's sake we shall not integrate it into the considerations of this chapter and because in practice such uncertainties in planning research, though recognized, are not formally taken into account. Simply speaking of the mathematical expectation of output, instead of using output straight away does not bring us much further.

3. Cf. Arrow (1962b).
4. For example the present discussion in The Netherlands of the internationalization of higher education and research can partly be described in terms of such a research climate.
5. See Samuelson (1954), (1955) and (1958). See also Peston (1972) and Head (1974).
6. See also Arrow (1962a) for a wider discussion of these issues.
7. The economies of scale in research facilities sometimes make for a certain 'free' availability for the 'local' researchers.
8. Sometimes it is possible to separate out results of such research which are 'secret', without completely spoiling the openness of a place. On the other hand, the immediate availability of prior local research results and a local research tradition may also lead to a certain narrowness.
9. Remarkably, this potential advantage has not always actually led to such cooperation but a discussion of the subtleties involved is beyond the scope of this chapter, which is primarily concerned with S & T cooperation. Some remarks on international cooperation in the social sciences are made in Waardenburg (1988).
10. While multilateral as well as bilateral arrangements are common in such cases, it is interesting to note which countries do not take part in such arrangements, since on the one hand exclusive 'clubs' may arise, while 'free rider' problems may surface where results are accessible to those not contributing to the research.
11. These remarks largely refer to several most useful papers in P.J. Lavakare et al. (1980).
12. See Oldham (1980). Though the observation is made in 1967, there is little reason to think that much has changed in these percentages since then.
13. This means that even full access for less developed countries (LDCs) to research results in developed countries (DCs) has only limited value because quite a few of these results cannot be appropriately applied in LDCs. The build-up of an indigenous research system is more important for LDCs.
14. Udgaonkar (1980) mentions that about half of all S & T manpower is engaged in military research.
15. See Oldham (1980).
16. A forceful, but extreme view from a Third World researcher on the dominance of the North in the field of research is given by S. Bandaranayake (1980). Many points in this chapter are supported in Streeten (1974).

REFERENCES

Arrow, K., 'Economic Welfare and the Allocation of Resources for Invention' in National Bureau of Economic Research, *The Rate and Direction of Inventure Activity: Economic and Social Factors*, Princeton University Press, Princeton, 1962a, pp. 609–25.
—— 'The Economic Implications of Learning by Doing', *Review of Economic Studies*, 29, 1962b; pp. 155–73.
—— 'Classificatory Notes on the Production and Transmission of Technological Knowledge', *American Economic Review Papers and Proceedings*, 59, 1969; pp. 29–35.
—— 'Knowledge, Productivity, and Practice', *Bulletin SEDELS*, Etude no. 909, suppl. 1965 (in French), translated in Arrow, K., *Collected Papers*, Vol. 5, 1985, pp. 191–9.
Bandaranayake, S., 'Control of Academics and Scientific Resources in Third

World Countries', in Lavakare *et al.*, op. cit., 1980.

Head, John G., *Public goods and Public welfare*, Duke University Press, Durham, 1974.

Lavakare, P.J., Ashok Parthasarathi, B.M. Udgaonkar (eds), *Scientific Cooperation for Development, Search for New Directions*, Vikas Publishing House, Sahibabad, India, 1980.

Marschak, Th., K. Glennan Jr., R. Summers, *Strategy for R & D: Studies in the Microeconomics of Development*, Springer, Berlin, 1967.

Nelson, R.R., 'The Simple Economics of Basic Scientific Research', *Journal of Political Economy* (1959), pp. 297–306.

Oldham, C.H.G., 'Reciprocity or Dependence', in Lavakare *et al.*, op. cit., 1980.

Peston, M., *Public Goods and the Public Sector*, Macmillan, London, 1972.

Samuelson, P.A., 'The Pure Theory of Public Expenditure', *Review of Economics and Statistics*, Nov. 1954, pp. 887–9.

—— 'Diagrammatic Exposition of a Theory of Public Expenditure', *Review of Economics and Statistics*, Nov. 1955, pp. 350–6.

—— 'Aspects of Public Expenditure Theories', *Review of Economics and Statistics*, Nov. 1958, pp. 332–8.

Solow, R.M., 'Technical Change and the Aggregate Production Function', *Review of Economics and Statistics*, 39, 1957, pp. 312–20.

Streeten, Paul P., 'Problems in the use and Transfer of an Intellectual Technology', *World Development*, Oct–Dec. 1974 (repr. in Lavakare *et al.*, op. cit., pp. 52–69.

Tinbergen, J., 'Zur Theorie der langfristligen Wirtschaftsentwicklung', *Weltwirtschaftliches Archiv* 55, 1942, pp. 511–49.

Udgaonkar, B.M., 'New Directions for International Scientific Cooperation', in Lavakare *et al.*, op. cit.

Waardenburg, J. George, 'Co-operation in Social Research', in Paul de Waart, Paul Peters and Erik Denters (eds), *International Law and Development*, Martinus Nijhoff, Dordrecht/Boston/London, 1988.

11 A science policy — some global concepts in the national context

P.J. Lavakare

INTRODUCTION

The fact that India and The Netherlands have jointly recognized the importance of science policy as a subject of relevance to their cooperation programme in science and technology shows the commitments of the two governments to consider collaborative Science and Technology activities in a planned manner based on national objectives and mutual understanding.

Any planning in science and technology has to take into account the activities and interests of individual scientists and technologists. Even though nowadays the planning, management and support of scientific activities is increasingly becoming the responsibility of governments, any bilateral collaborative programme in Science Policy will meet with certain disaster if it ignores the dominant role played by individual Scientists and Technologists in such a collaborative venture. The ideal composition of the collaborating teams must therefore be a mix of professional scientists and engineers, social scientists, economists and planners, who are all important partners in the programme of formulation and implementation of a science policy.

Having recognized the role of scientists and engineers, one must hasten to add that governments now also have a major responsibility in financing and promoting science and technology activities. In this context there is a definite need for setting down clear-cut objectives and policy guidelines for promoting science and technology activities as part of national and international developmental programmes; the policies relating to science and technology activities have to be laid down by governments with the involvement of all concerned.

In planning for S & T activities, financial investment decisions necessarily become an important element of policy considerations for any government. But in doing so, it must realize that scientific activities cannot be looked at as a short-term investment like a business enterprise, for these investments are going to give returns of a different kind, and necessarily on a long-term basis. This is particularly true for a developing country like India where the aspirations of the people, their desire to make a creative contribution and their natural curiosity and thirst for knowledge — knowledge not necessarily for economic benefits but knowledge to maintain their spirit — form the key to national prosperity. In the effort to satisfy these aspirations, it is necessary to have a policy which will support, integrate and develop a sound infrastructure for pursuing science and technology activities within the country. At the same time the general principles for providing support to science and technology should also aspire to secure for the people of the country all the benefits that can accrue from the acquisition and application of scientific knowledge. This was essentially the approach of the government of India when it formulated its Scientific Policy Resolution in March 1958.[1] This policy clearly identifies India's commitment to the challenging activity of utilizing science and technology for national development.

Recognizing the importance which has to be given by any government to a rational science policy, it goes without saying that it has to have a very strong political support to pursue such a policy. The papers discussed in this Indo–Dutch debate have clearly identified the strong political support that both countries have given to their commitment to utilize science and technology for national development. Right from the days of its first Prime Minister, Pandit Jawaharlal Nehru, then through his illustrious daughter, Shrimati Indira Gandhi and now through the young prime minister Shri Rajiv Gandhi, India's leaders have all developed and supported science and technology activities. The portfolio of Science and Technology has always been attached to the Office of the Prime Minister. What more political support can one expect?

SOME ELEMENTS OF A SCIENCE POLICY

Having accepted science and technology as an important tool for national development, a science policy must clearly take account of the following four elements:

(a) The need to foster, promote and sustain the cultivation of science and *scientific research* in all its aspects — pure, applied and educational.
(b) The element of *social development* through the provision of goods and services and the provision of basic needs such as food, housing, communication, etc. and also to foster a 'scientific attitude' in the people.
(c) *Economic development*, manifested through a rapidly growing and indigenous industrial development which would not only provide the requisite products, but also employment and contributions to capital formation.
(d) *The national security* through meaningful application of science and technology and the use of these tools for maintaining peace and security.

It is not possible to go into the details of each of these facets of development where science and technology would play an increasingly important role. Various chapters in this book by authors from India and The Netherlands, have covered many of these aspects in some detail. No doubt the two societies have a different developmental background; one being a large developing country and the other a very small developed country. In India we have always recognized that pure science is an international activity which has to be pursued following international standards, but the technology developed through the application of science has to be utilized for national development in the context of national needs and the social ethos.

Having stated some of the basic concepts involved in a science policy, both in a global and a national context, it becomes imperative for a country to outline its national goals and priorities clearly and incorporate these elements into specific programmes of national development, utilizing the tools of science and technology. W.J. Deetman stated that 'Policy can help to ensure that science and technology are instruments to serve people and not the other way around. It should be instrumental not only for us in The Netherlands today but also for the use of future generations and the people of the third world.'[2] If this spirit of a global science policy is accepted then the development of the world as a whole would be much more simple. Unfortunately, such a universal concept has not yet been applied uniformly throughout the world. The question of setting priorities becomes very country specific and the same tools may have to be used differently in different situations. If the objective of Indian socio-economic development highlights the eradication of poverty through provision of basic human needs like food, we must focus on the problems of increasing our food production through modern techniques to improve the quality of life. Luxuries available through modern technological developments may have to be given a lower priority until the basic needs have been given adequate attention. This does not imply that our programmes have to be limited only to using and pursuing those tools of S & T which have immediate benefits. A balanced growth in various areas of S & T, some of which may have unexpected spin-offs, cannot be ignored. Speaking at the 71st session of the Indian Science Congress held in 1984, Indira Gandhi, while highlighting the importance of improving the quality of Indian Science, has said: 'basic research cannot be starved, for it attracts the best scientists and has yielded unexpected spin-offs even in unattempted applications'.

It is this balance in development of S & T which becomes in essence the crux of a science policy in determining national priorities. The nexus between pursuit of basic research and its possible utilization by any society cannot be predictably established. We in India feel that a creative society has necessarily to be cultivated, recognizing it as a fundamental right of the people. For that reason as far as basic research is concerned, one cannot establish priorities on the basis of social criteria. What one does is to judge its quality and to a certain extent, its efficiency in the scientific sense. Professor H.G. van Bueren has emphasized this aspect when he said that 'creativity cannot be controlled'.[3]

In the case of economic development through industrial growth, while it appears to be a globally accepted solution, we are often faced with the problem of choice of technology for industrial development — the dilemma of using indigenously developed technology versus technology imported from abroad. These issues do not have a global solution, but have to be looked at, and solved, only in the national context. The arguments which may be valid for The Netherlands importing a technology may not be at all relevant for the same technology being imported by India, hence the choices and priorities have to be based on individual national considerations. These choices have to be based on extensive discussions not only among scientists and policymakers within the country but sometimes also with the international community as required. The global concept of industrial development through use of S & T has to be understood in the national context.

SOME GLOBAL ISSUES AND CHOICES

The most important choices and priorities which have to be made in the context of utilizing S & T are in the difficult realm of security and peace. On the one hand the development of S & T and its extensive use for solving the problems of mankind have been most admirable, but on the other, we have seen the irrational and lethal use of these same tools for destroying large sections of mankind. It is not the inherent knowledge that has emerged from scientific and technological pursuit that has to be blamed, but the choices and priorities which man has set in utilizing these tools which have to be questioned. There is a famous Buddhist proverb which says: 'To every man is given the key to the gates of heaven; the same key opens the gates of hell.' A science policy should therefore clearly indicate a nation's desire for using S & T for the ultimate benefit of mankind.

In India we have always believed in using S & T for peaceful purposes and our policies have always reflected this desire. We have even raised our voices at major global forums and called for a programme of global disarmament so that the tools of development resulting from the pursuit of challenging areas like nuclear science and atomic energy would no longer be used for purposes to which they are increasingly being diverted. We believe in using atoms for peace and not for destruction, and we feel that a science policy should emphasize all these elements which will bring about security and peace not only for individual countries but for the world as a whole.

Another issue which has a certain global character relates to the fact that effective use of S & T very much depends upon the indigenous capacity of an individual country, both in terms of expertise to develop knowledge and effectively to apply the acquired knowledge. As a result of a series of debates at international forums, in particular at the UN Conference on Science and Technology for Development held in Vienna in August 1979, a consensus emerged that the developing countries must build up an endogenous capability for problem solving, decisionmaking and implementation in all matters related to S & T for development. This capability which, to a certain extent, is the essence of self-reliance, includes a capacity to adapt, generate, utilize and diffuse knowledge acquired through pursuit of S & T with relevance to national development objectives. Since the developing countries cover a wide spectrum of socio-economic backgrounds and are at various stages of development, it will once again not be adequate to define a common approach for all the developing countries. Individual countries have to look at their own national needs and priorities and if they conclude that S & T should be the tools for their national development, they will have to develop this endogenous capability through conscious efforts involving a national commitment through a science policy. In the world today, more than 95 per cent of R & D efforts are concentrated in developed countries and, as a result, the developing countries are not able fully and effectively to utilize the global developments in S & T because their own efforts at understanding the capabilities of S & T have so far been very limited. In a sense 95 per cent of the knowledge developed outside the realm of developing countries is 'available' for individual national development, but the very nature of its foreign origin causes a certain number of developmental constraints which could be considerably reduced if only the indigenous S & T capacity of a country were strengthened so that global knowledge can be meaningfully selected and applied in individual national contexts. It does become imperative that science policies of individual countries whose objective is to use S & T for development will have to stress the importance of endogenous capability building. This element of science policy is often not recognized when global pressures are put on developing countries to import foreign technologies. This is not to say that internationally available fruits of S & T are not relevant for use by the developing countries, but the emphasis must be on ensuring that their application and use is done in an environment which is conducive to fulfilling national objectives.

It is in this context of using internationally available knowledge that the process of international collaboration among various countries, including that between developed and developing, becomes important. The process of international collaboration in S & T is not merely a trading relation of give and take, involving products and services. It involves cooperation between partners who have to keep in mind mutuality of interest. No doubt one partner is endowed better than the other but this should not allow him to exploit the other because of this imbalance. The ultimate objective must be to share experience and capabilities and try to ensure that both benefit equitably. A developing country can benefit through an international collaboration only if it will enable it to stand on its own feet in the long run. The problem of repetitive import of technology which has proven to be detrimental to the economic growth of the importing country is well known and efforts must be made to avoid such phenomena. The only way to ensure this is through the commitment of an individual country, through its S & T policies, to ensure that gradually its capacity to absorb and innovate its own technological requirements is increased. The importance of international cooperation in S & T for development has been rightly stressed by a group of Pugwash scientists through the evolution of 'Guidelines for International Cooperation' which have given, in detail, the international perspective for national development through S & T.[4] This element of international cooperation defined through the Pugwash guidelines should form an important element of the science policy of an individual country.

Every policymaker at some stage has to come to some quantitative decisons, particularly when it comes to financial investments. Science and technology is one area where adequate attention has not been given globally to defining the optimum input required for maximal benefits for development. International comparisons of R & D investments are often given as a percentage of GNP and while it is generally seen that developed countries contribute more than 2–3 per cent of their GNP for R & D activities, most of the developing countries contribute significantly less than 1 per cent of their already meagre GNP. While there is no yardstick yet known which defines an optimum percentage of GNP which should be committed to R & D activities, these figures tend to indicate the dividing line between the developing and the developed countries. No science policy has been able to define what this target should be but if the gap between developed and developing countries is to be reduced rapidly, to start with the developing countries would have to accept, as part of their science policy, a commitment that at least 1–2 per cent of their GNP be devoted towards R & D activities. The need for such a guideline is, at the present moment, necessary for most developing countries. It is quite likely that as a result of major developments in S & T, the strategies for development in developed countries will drastically change this figure in future, but the global trends are very clear and the need for reflecting these in the national Science Policies of the developing countries cannot be denied.

IMPLEMENTATION OF S & T POLICIES

While these elements of global S & T policies may appear to have some general characteristics, implementation at the national level requires a considerable amount of understanding of the national socio-economic and cultural scene. Merely to say that S & T should form part of the socio-cultural ethos may mean different things to different people. In a Western society, science has already percolated into the lives of the people. The concepts of S & T are, to a considerable extent, accepted and therefore it becomes easier for the governments to pursue programmes involving the application of S & T with the full cooperation, participation and support of society. In the Indian context, Pandit Jawaharlal Nehru was concerned very much with this issue when he noted that there was a lack of what he called the 'scientific temper' in the Indian population at large. Although Indian society is culturally very rich, to understand the developmental role of science it would be important to accept the tools of S & T, and this would be difficult for a vast proportion of the Indian people. This attitude is not restricted to the economically poor or uneducated, but the 'scientific temper' is seen lacking even in the best of elites and sometimes even in those who are practising science. Pandit Nehru felt that this was a major obstacle to the application of S & T for development. In order to overcome this obstacle, he decided to formulate a Scientific Policy Resolution which he got approved by the Parliament in March 1958. Such a national commitment to the pursuit of S & T in various facets of national development was indeed the best way of initiating the process of implementation of S & T policies in a developing country. As a result of this commitment, while the government has increasingly enhanced S & T activities in the country (the R & D as a percentage of GNP has grown from about 0.6 per cent during 1978–9 to 1.1 per cent in 1986–7), the share of the private sector has not been as large as one would like, certainly not approaching what one sees in the developed countries. A commitment to R & D in the industrial sector, and even more so in the private sector, is considerably lacking and the total impact of the S & T policies cannot be seen unless and until there is a full involvement of the various sectors where science and technology percolates; education, research, industry and socio-economic sectors of development.

Apart from the commitment of resources to S & T activities, there is a greater need for emphasizing effective management of S & T activities carried out at different levels in society. The quality of S & T education, the pursuit of excellence in the research field, an application of modern techniques in efficient management of industry and full utilization of natural resources through appropriate use of S & T are some of the areas where greater emphasis and attention needs to be focused. While it is recognized that academic activities need a certain amount of free environment and cannot be always 'managed' through planning techniques like PERT, an emphasis on selectivity, prioritization and quality control cannot be ignored. Even where there are time-bound projects involving application and utilization of technology, one sees a certain amount of slackness resulting in decreased productivity. Increasingly greater attention is being given to aspects of management of S & T and concepts such as undertaking 'technology missions' and implementing projects in a 'mission mode' are being discussed and specific time-bound programmes drawn up on that basis. It is this aspect of implementing the S & T policy that needs greater attention in India and other developing countries. Such an implementation mechanism must be coupled with professional studies, whether they relate to technology information, or technology forecasting and assessment, which can give a certain amount of direction and help in long-term planning for S & T activities. Further, S & T activities are very often isolated and those carried out in academic institutions never percolate down to socio-economic sectors or production sectors. Such lack of linkages has been one of the banes of the Indian S & T scene and this gulf will further decelerate the process of economic growth through the application of S & T, if not properly attended to.

Finally one cannot but look at S & T without being influenced by a certain amount of personal involvement and some personal experiences and observations which accumulate through a long association with science and its international character. Scientists are very often considered as being isolated or being aloof from the finer aspects of human activity, namely, the fine arts. But I have always believed that a full appreciation of science and its relevance to society could happen only if the scientists have a global exposure to the world of art as well. My first infatuation with The Netherlands was through one such association. During my graduate student days in the United States, I was, for the first time, exposed to the massive work of the famous Dutch artist Vincent Van Gogh, which, today, haunts me as I visit art galleries in Europe, the United States and even in India. I was particularly impressed by the famous letters written by Van Gogh who clearly expressed his feelings not only through colours but through a personal understanding and perhaps suffering of humanity. Describing his well-known painting entitled 'The Night Cafe' he has said: 'I have tried to express the terrible passions of humanity by means of red and green,' and he continued to describe another famous painting also depicting a cafe at night when he said: 'the night is more alive and more richly coloured than the day.'

I always felt that these utterances of Van Gogh bring out clearly his concerns for humanity even when he was deeply involved in his professional activities. I hope all the professions, whether they relate to science, technology or business would keep this element of humanity in the forefront of their activities.

As a space scientist, working at the Tata institute of Fundamental Research, I was soon exposed to the lectures of the famous Dutch astrophysicist Professor Van de Hulst and thus a new association with Dutch Science began. This association soon took me to different towns in The Netherlands, both big and small. My visits to The Netherlands not only exposed me to the famous art galleries of Amsterdam and its waterways, but the artistic Dutch windmills and the pleasing aroma of the Dutch cigars soon became an attraction in each of my subsequent visits. However, my last professional visit was perhaps the most memorable one, when I participated in the 30th Pugwash Conference on Science and World Affairs which was held in the small town of Breukelen during August 1980. This small town was visited by about 150 scientists from thirty-eight countries all over the world to express their concern over the growing dangers of a nuclear war — a danger which has its origin in the uncontrolled developments in science and technology. How soon a 'sane' Science Policy will curb this danger, I do not know, but I think the voices raised in Breukelen in 1980 can perhaps be echoed again and again and I hope that scientists will continue to pay attention to the question of peace in this exciting world of science and technology.

And finally, let me end my remarks by a quotation from our late Prime Minister Indira Gandhi when she addressed the 61st Session of the Indian Science Congress in 1974, which in my view, truly reflects our own approach and policy of self-reliance in the pursuit of Science and Technology:

Let us in India certainly benefit from the experiences and discoveries of foreign Scientists and Technologists, for there should be no boundaries for knowledge. But let our minds not be imprisoned by foreign points of view.

NOTES

1. The Scientific Policy Resolution, Government of India, 1958.
2. W.J. Deetman, *Science Policy*, Vol. II, p. 16, February 1989.
3. H.G. Van Bueren, *Science Policy*, Vol. II, p. 19, February 1989.
4. 'Scientific Co-operation for Development — Search for New Directions', P.J. Lavakare, Ashok Parthasarathi, B.M. Udgaonkar (eds), Vikas, New Delhi, 1980.

12 Some problems in international scientific cooperation

C.M. Cooper

An economist's perceptions of the nature of knowledge, particularly scientific knowledge, may be of some help in understanding the nature and limits of international cooperation in science and technology. This chapter is based on ideas which are well established in economics.

A first point to note is that knowledge is in principle a 'free good' in economic parlance. Knowledge shares with some other phenomena the curious property that it is not diminished by being consumed. In other words the use of some piece of knowledge by an additional person does not impose a cost on society. This is never strictly true of course but it is an acceptable approximation for the purposes of exposition. If one accepts this, it must follow that from the 'social' point of view of welfare economics the 'optimum' price for knowledge is just zero. The 'consumption' of knowledge will be less than is socially desirable if a non-zero price is charged for it.

Quite a lot of the knowledge with which the Indo–Dutch conference on science policy is concerned is in fact exchanged internationally at something close to a zero price — more strictly at a price which is determined simply by the mechanics of transferring it from one country to another or from one institution to another. This is the case, for example, with many results in basic scientific research which are mainly transferred through the scientific journals, or through exchanges of information between institutes and faculties.

It is obvious though that not all scientific and technical knowledge is in fact exchanged at zero cost in this sense. Even in basic sciences there are often important scientific discoveries which are withheld from normal circulation because, for example, of their strategic economic, political or military importance in the country in which they are made. And outside the basic sciences, in applied science and technology the costs of obtaining knowledge can be very high; here knowledge has a high price and so in a strict sense it will be under-utilized.

The free-good nature of knowledge in fact gives rise to a basic contradiction. Although the social opportunity cost of a further use of knowledge (and hence its optimum price) is zero, it always costs resources, and often a very large amount of resources, to create it. This gives rise to a nasty practical problem, since if all new knowledge were priced by edict at the socially optimal level of zero, no private economic agent would ever be interested in creating it. Why should an individual or a firm spend a large amount of money to make scientific discoveries if they are prevented from selling what they find out at a price which gives them a normal return on their outlays? So while the optimum price of knowledge — measured by the social opportunity cost of using it — should be zero, in practice, if it were everywhere so, there would be a general underinvestment in its creation. One cannot have it both ways.

This argument is familiar as the main rationale for state intervention in the creation of knowledge, especially through fundamental research activities in the universities and state institutes. In certain sectors the state finances the creation of new knowledge precisely because it is considered desirable for one reason or another that in these fields at least the price of the knowledge to the wider world should be zero — and its use thus more or less optimal.[1] In addition the state has involved itself for the more workaday reason that the widening of fundamental scientific knowledge is widely held to be necessary to the ultimate generation of technologies in production, defence and the like.

In those fields where the state is not directly active and the creation of new knowledge is left to the action of private economic agents, there will be no incentives to finance the search for it unless the agents perceive opportunities for economic advantage from having it. In general this requires that they are able to restrict the dissemination of new knowledge — at least for a time — so as to gain special advantages from its unique possession. Where the knowledge in question is about production, this implies secrecy or patent protection so as to support a 'quasi-monopoly' in its use, which in turn will result in some degree of monopoly in the product market. In such cases, although the 'social cost' of more widespread use of the knowledge is still zero — there are very real private costs to the agents who generated the knowledge in the first place in making it available to others. These private costs result from the loss of revenues and profits which would have been obtained if the dissemination had not taken place. In general as is well known, firms and individuals normally only make such knowledge available if they are paid for it at a price which covers the perceived cost of these forgone profits. Such transactions are by nature very complex and involve contractual agreements. They are customarily misleadingly described as 'transfers' of technology. More precisely, they are commercial agreements to share the degree of monopoly power and the associated profits which the knowledge in question confers. There is no serious possibility that this type of 'appropriated' knowledge will exchange at anything near an optimum (zero) price until it has been so widely imitated that there is no longer a premium attached to its use.

In fields where the creation of knowledge has come to depend on the possibility of its appropriation, international cooperation in the limited and strict sense with which we are concerned is not really in question. International exchanges will continue to be done on commercial terms; governments, particularly in the receiving countries will, if they are sensible, look for ways of monitoring and controlling what is going on. India of course has a considerable state apparatus for doing this.

It is important to note however, that these restrictive and inherently commercial exchanges of knowledge are not necessarily characteristic of all productive sectors. In the agricultural sectors for example, a large part of scientific knowledge has customarily been generated by state research institutes in the First World as well as in the Third.[2] This happens for well-known reasons. Where there are many small producers, the chances of appropriating knowledge are slender, and it is anyway unlikely that individual producers will be able to assemble the resources needed to support the research required.

One obvious implication of this is that it is important to recognize the limits to international scientific cooperation in its normal, non-commercial forms. It is customarily confined to areas of research in which the state has a high degree of control because it is the paymaster. This can include research directed to the productive sectors (like agriculture). It can also include research on public utilities ancillary to production where these are in state control. It would indeed be interesting if there were more research on 'fringe areas' where for example governments collaborate with commercial knowledge creators so as to induce more international collaboration. Some of this might happen in aid programmes.

However, the point of these remarks is to indicate problems that may be expected to arise in the near future — especially the possibility that fields of action for international scientific cooperation may be narrowed down in the future. There are at least three reasons why commercial appropriation of knowledge may expand in the future and invade the traditional fields of action of international scientific cooperation.

First, developments in the organization of production in some sectors of the industrialized economies have expanded the area on which knowledge is created on commercial terms. The most obvious instance has been the emergence of industrialized agriculture, dominated increasingly by large firms carrying out research on more or less the same terms as in the oligopolized industrial sectors. Expansion of plantation production systems usually has the same effect.

Second, it seems likely that technological developments themselves will expand the areas in which appropriated knowledge is important. From the Indian standpoint the most important are probably the developments in biotechnology where firms, individuals and university departments are seeking with considerable success to appropriate potentially vital fundamental scientific knowledge. Developments in this field could result in a transformation of our traditional perceptions of basic scientific enquiry and its purposes. This is probably part of a more general pushing back of the boundary between state-supported 'pure' science and commercially-orientated science as the time lags between fundamental discoveries and commercial application have shortened.

Third, and conceivably most important, the institutional setting for fundamental research in much of the industrialized world is being steadily transformed as a matter of government policy. The reductions of public expenditures on universities in Europe — especially perhaps in the United Kingdom — have resulted in a general search for commercial sponsorship. This is shifting the university research profile towards more applied problems. It has also increased the amount of confidential contract research being done in European universities.

All of these developments imply closer links between fundamental science and production, and a corresponding increase in the fields where appropriation of knowledge is central to the incentive to create it. There are of course different views about the desirability of these developments. That, however, is not the immediate point. More relevant to our concerns is the fact that these developments either imply a narrowing of the traditional fields of action of international scientific cooperation, or some significant transformation of its content. As far as I am aware there is not much research being done on these questions.

NOTES

1. There are of course fields — like military research — in which state finance of research is done for quite different reasons.
2. The plantation sectors are however more like the industrial sectors, in the way knowledge creation is done, and knowledge is appropriated.

Discussion summary

Rais Ahmed

There are several issues that came up for discussion on the international dimension of R & D and international cooperation. It was obvious that the present highly uneven development of science as between Western Europe and the United States on the one hand, and the ex-colonial countries which largely today constitute the newly independent and the so-called developing countries on the other hand is a result of several historical factors. Post-Second-World-War developments have, however, not helped to bridge the gap. If anything the gap has increased: and given the way international relationships in R & D, in industry and trade — and in the context of the cold war — operate there is little prospect of the gap being bridged. It is widely believed, however, by the scientific community that increasingly acute problems of underdevelopment, namely explosive population growth, depletion of natural resources, environmental degradation, etc. accompanied by poverty, undernourishment and lack of education are bound to hurt the developed countries too. Peace and stability in the world cannot be secured if this asymmetry of development continues.

Science and technology, or research and development, have a great potential to play a positive role, but only if the countries concerned design their economic and social goals and policies so as to take advantage of this potential. If a minimum human needs programme is worked out, consequent tasks in all sectors, including R & D could be evolved. But, world experience with such a complex venture is very limited. This question has been discussed at various forums, but designing and modelling a system on this basis has scarcely been undertaken. There is considerable appreciation of the difficulties which developing countries experience in the present framework. The desirability for a freer flow of scientific knowledge was accepted, but economic pressure for emphasizing priority rights and strategic constraints on this free flow as well as the negative impact of this pressure on the growth of science and on its use for welfare, especially in developing countries, was recognized (even though with an expression of helplessness). The need for R & D efforts in all countries to be consistent with peace and stability was appreciated and the need to build an indigenous research system in developing countries through political will and international cooperation was underscored.

In exploring areas of cooperation for the greatest benefit to India and The Netherlands, as well as between other developing and developed countries, the desirability of seminars on the nature of scientific knowledge and its relation to cultural, social and economic development was suggested. Cooperation in basic research, through individual participation as well as that among research groups and institutions was considered to be important, particularly since this sphere is least encumbered with constraints. Other spheres of cooperation could be in specific projects such as, perhaps, establishing data and analytical systems for scientific and technical activity, and in technology assessment and forecasting.

It was recognized that while new knowledge generated through international cooperation may be exploited by both partners, the diverse infrastructure which exists in the developed and the developing countries may result in the possibility of one country exploiting the knowledge more efficiently than the others. Cooperation agreements must take these differences into account. The developed countries also have certain commitments to industry and cannot force their industries to share their knowledge openly with the developing countries. The element of cooperation, if it involves industry, would have to take this fact into account when finalizing cooperative agreements. To this extent there are limitations to international cooperation in R & D and to avoid misunderstanding between the partners, they must be openly discussed and understood by both sides. Cooperation involving industry is thus different from that involving academic institutions only.

Part V: Country reports

13 Science and technology policies in India*

AN OVERVIEW OF SCIENCE POLICY

Science and technology (S & T) in India has grown under a strong and sustained political support. Even before India became independent in 1947, the national leaders had recognized the role of S & T in national development. After independence, Jawaharlal Nehru, the first prime minister of India, played a leading role in laying down foundations of S & T in India. Political awareness of the importance of science in the nation-building process was generated. He also ensured the establishment of a wide-based infrastructure for S & T through deep personal involvement. S & T under Nehru's vision came to be accepted as an instrument not only for industrial and economic development but also for transforming a tradition-bound society into a dynamic and progressive nation. The Constitution of India adopted in 1950[1] reflects this political vision. The directive principles and the fundamental duties outlined in the constitutional state: 'It shall be the duty of every citizen of India to develop Scientific Temper, humanism and spirit of inquiry and reform.'

The Scientific Policy Resolution (SPR) adopted by the Parliament in 1958,[2] the first enunciation of the government's approach to S & T, reflected this vision. The understanding of S & T by the political leadership of that time continues to shape the present policies and plans. As recently as January 1983, the government enunciated its policies on technology through the announcement of the Technology Policy Statement (TPS).[3] Combined with the concept of socialism, the state continues to be a strong supporter of S & T, providing 80 per cent of funds for all research and development undertaken in the country. It also shoulders responsibility for directly guiding and planning the activities of an extensive network of S & T institutions.

Though the basic orientation of national S & T policy has been, and still is, to treat science and technology as an integral part of socio-economic development, there have been several changes in the organization and planning strategies over the years. These changes have, generally, directed S & T from an infrastructure and capability-building phase (1947 to 1960s) to assessment and reorientation (1970 to 1980s), on to an account on performance and accountability. We shall briefly discuss these changes.

---

*This report has been prepared under the supervision of Dr Ashok Jain, Director, National Institute of Science, Technology and Development Studies (NISTADS), New Delhi.

Nurturing of infrastructure

From 1947 until the late sixties, S & T infrastructure was established and nurtured for building up research capabilities on a broad basis. It was considered premature to put demands on S & T to contribute to specific developmental problems either in industry or agriculture. Investments in S & T were essentially for creating assets in the form of manpower and infrastructure that would, in due course, become available for addressing the needs of the country. Policy instruments and planning mechanisms linking S & T to socio-economic plans were kept flexible. The plans emphasized development of agriculture and modern industry but the immediate shortage of food grain was met through imports; modernization of industry was based on foreign technology and investments. The Industrial Policy Resolution of 1948[4] allowed considerable scope for introducing foreign technology into the country, but had little to say on linking the imports with indigenous S & T infrastructure. The favourable sterling balance accumulated during the war enabled a relaxed view on imports on one hand, and the Scientific Policy Resolution with emphasis on spirit of free enquiry allowed for independent growth of S & T on the other. Under this policy ethos, an extensive research infrastructure came into existence within a period of twenty years, almost undisturbed by the successes and failures on the economic front. The priorities in S & T were influenced by the leaders of science in whom the political leadership committed to science had trust and faith. Efforts at formulating policy instruments and plans to couple S & T capabilities with requirements of agriculture, industry and other economic sectors remained weak.

Assessment and reorientation phase

By the late 1960s, the expectation that research institutions should manifestly contribute to economic development started finding expression in the mass media, Parliament and other forums. There were several factors that led to this situation. Despite the open-door policy for foreign investments and technology imports, the extent of such investments in certain sectors had remained low. For example, areas like exportation of oil and gas, steel, major-sized capital goods, heavy machinery, basic organic chemicals, etc. were not considered viable by foreign investors, perhaps due to lack of confidence in the available technical manpower, future growth prospects and economic stability. In addition, food imports for a rising population, conflicts with China in 1962 and with Pakistan in 1965 meant depletion of the sterling balance. It was also realized that modalities of technology imports adopted thus far had contributed little to the enhancement of indigenous technological capabilities. In general, investment decisions came under critical review and in this context it was felt that linkages between the research infrastructure and the socio-economic system had to be strengthened. During the 1970s, therefore, science policy and plans came in for a re-examination and reorientation. A National Committee on Science and

Technology (NCST), set up in 1973, prepared, for the first time, a plan for science and technology derived from the priorities of economic development.[5] A separate department of science and technology was created to follow up these plans and programmes in consultation with the Planning Commission. Agricultural research was reorganized and expanded to cover activities ranging from research, manpower generation, extension down to the training of farmers. A Science and Engineering Research Council (SERC) was set up to promote front-line research in emerging and inter-disciplinary areas. Project funding to the universities during this period increased several fold through SERC ensuring a high degree of selectivity (a rejection rate of 70–80 per cent).[6] On the industrial front also important policy changes were made that had a strong influence on the utilization of indigenous R & D capabilities. Import of technology came under modified regulations through the Foreign Investment Board and the Industrial Licensing Policy Instruments. Industries were classified into categories where foreign collaboration was or was not allowed. This enabled the research institutions to direct their efforts in areas where foreign technology was not likely to be introduced. Thus 'import-substitution' became the focal theme for R & D efforts. Simultaneously the Indian Patent Act was introduced in 1970. This allowed only processes to be patented in sectors like food, medicine, drugs and chemical substances. A package of extraordinary incentives to promote in-house R & D in industry was introduced in the form of tax incentives. Write-offs of 100 per cent on capital investments for R & D, and 133 per cent for expenditure on sponsored research were made available to industry.

The above changes introduced during the 1970s had a strong influence on the S & T structure in India. S & T plans became an integral part of the five-year planning exercise.[7] In several areas, indigenous research moved up to production, for example in electronics, drugs and pharmaceuticals, pesticides, chemicals, power generating equipment, agriculture and food processing. A large number of in-house R & D units were established in industry.[8] Capabilities in new areas like non-conventional sources of energy, ocean resources, environment, new-materials, communication and informatics, space applications, remote sensing, fast-breeder reactor technology and bio-technology were established. Sophisticated equipment for front-line research became available to universities on a fairly extensive scale. Self-sufficiency in food grains had been achieved. It became possible to bargain for reduced payments for technology imports and also indigenously develop parts of technology in the form of detailed engineering and introduce procurement inspection and construction through Indian engineering consultancy organizations.[9]

ACCENT ON ACCOUNTABILITY AND PERFORMANCE

The reorientation of policies and plans initiated during the 1970s started putting additional demands on S & T. Since the 1980s the capabilities in S & T, built over four decades of independence, are perceived to have matured to a stage where R & D programmes can be conceived and executed covering the entire innovation chain, that is from invention to innovation to diffusion or delivery of specific products and services. Under this ethos, technology acquired a stronger focus, accountability and questions relating to returns on investments in S & T became important. The Technology Policy Statement of 1983, that came twenty-five years after the Scientific Policy Resolution, reflects this change. The launching of six technology missions in a short period of three years (1985–8) for meeting the immediate needs for drinking water, literacy, edible oils, immunization, rural communication and dairy products have been manifestations of the accent on accountability and performance.[10] The setting up of a Technology Development Fund and risk investment mechanisms within the financial institutions and of science and technology advisory committees in economic ministries are also steps towards forging stronger linkages between R & D and economic activities.

The S & T policy and planning in India since 1947 is thus seen to have retained the overall goal orientation contained in the Scientific Policy Resolution, viz., 'in general, to secure for the people of the country all the benefits that can accrue from the acquisition and application of scientific knowledge'. In terms of approach and strategy, however, there have been significant changes. It has been an evolutionary process with policies for the development of agriculture, industry and in general the direction of socio-economic development exerting a strong influence on S & T policies and plans. A sustained and continuous political support for S & T has enabled the system to evolve without sudden jerks and jolts.

ORGANIZATION OF SCIENCE AND TECHNOLOGY

The structures for carrying out S & T activities are organized on the basis of policies and strategies for integrating S & T with socio-economic goals. The two policy statements of 1958 and 1983, mentioned above, refer specifically to the directions which scientific endeavours and technological developments are to take, other policies of the government strongly influence the organization of S & T. For example, the Industrial Policy Resolution,[4] the Industrial Act and related policies and legislations — the health policy, the electronics policy, the computer policy, the education policy, etc. — play an important role in determining structures concerned with development of technology. Indeed, unlike scientific research, development of indigenous capabilities in technology and their utilization are influenced to a large extent by policies relating to importation of technology, strategies adopted for industrial growth, the role assigned to private- and public-sector undertakings, etc. Thus, in general, 'technology policy' necessarily has closer links with the policies relating to socio-economic development as compared to 'Science Policy'.

The S & T organizational framework is shown in Figure 13.1. The prime minister has always been the minister-in-charge for science and technology. For this he has three advisory mechanisms: the scientific adviser, the adviser for technology missions, and an independent eleven-

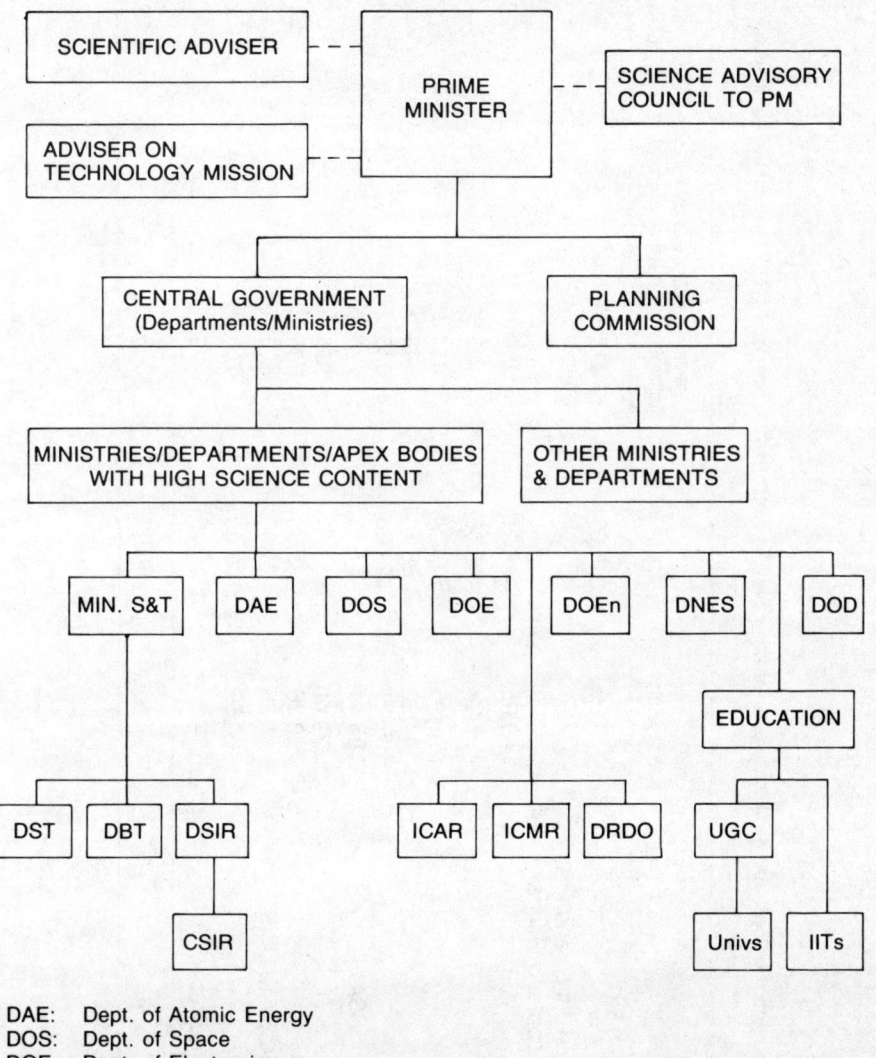

DAE: Dept. of Atomic Energy
DOS: Dept. of Space
DOE: Dept. of Electronics
DOEn: Dept. of Environment
DNES: Dept. of Non-conventional Energy Sources
DOD: Dept. of Ocean Development
DBT: Dept. of Biotechnology
DST: Dept. of Science & Technology
DSIR: Dept. of Scientific and Industrial Research
ICMR: Indian Council of Medical Research
ICAR: Indian Council of Agricultural Research
DRDO: Defence Research and Development Organisation
CSIR: Council of Scientific and Industrial Research
UGC: University Grants Commission
IIT: Indian Institutes of Technology
Univs: Universities

Figure 13.1   Science and technology framework of central government

Table 13.1a S & T expenditure for the sixth five-year plan and outlays for the seventh five-year plan 1985–1990 (S & T sectors) (in Rs. crores)*

Sectors	sixth five-year plan	total	seventh plan outlays 1985–1990 central government	states	UTs
1. Atomic Energy (S & T)	234.59	315.00	315.00	—	—
2. Environment and ecology; prevention and control of air and water pollution and Ganga action plan	40.05	427.91	350.00	75.71	2.20
3. Ocean development (S & T)	87.04	100.00	100.00	—	—
4. Dept. of Science & Techn.	269.93	543.09	458.43	81.57	3.09
a. Meteorology	47.22	88.78	88.78	—	—
b. S & T-programmes	137.27	429.66	345.00	81.57	3.09
c. Meteorology component of INSAT	85.44	24.65	24.65	—	—
5. Scientific and industrial research	221.71	355.00	355.00	—	—
a. CSIR	220.36	335.00	335.00	—	—
b. Schemes transferred from DST to DSIR	1.35	20.00	20.00	—	—
6. Space (S & T)	304.56	700.00	700.00	—	—
7. Forensic science and police wireless	—	25.00	25.00	—	—
TOTAL	1157.88	2466.00	2303.43	157.28	5.29

*crore = 10 million Rs.

Table 13.1b S & T expenditure for the sixth plan and outlays for the seventh plan (socio-economic sectors) (Rs. crores)

Sectors	Sixth plan (1980–5)	Seventh plan (1985–90) (outlays)
1. Agriculture research (ICAR)	287.10	425.00
2. Biomedical research (ICMR)	48.08	150.00
3. Chemicals and fertilizers	14.76	—
4. Civil aviation	0.96	3.47
5. Coal	6.15	120.00
6. Communications	40.57	—
7. Drugs and pharmaceuticals	*	7.00
8. Education	—	180.00
9. Electronics	21.05	—
10. Food and civil supplies	3.71	18.28
11. Forest and wild life	10.78	—
12. Heavy industry	40.00	—
13. Housing	—	3.00
14. Industrial development	23.73	—
15. Information and broadcasting	1.80	—
16. Irrigation development and water management	12.37	10.00
17. Labour	0.36	1.51
18. Mines	14.18	30.24
19. National test house	7.11	14.75
20. Non-conventional energy sources	44.00	—
21. Petroleum and petrochemicals	67.40	191.74
22. Power	28.45	—
23. Railways	—	—
24. Rural development	15.02	20.00
25. Shipping and transport	3.50	—
26. Social welfare and nutrition	1.04	—
27. Steel	59.91	—
28. Textiles	—	—

Notes: As information on S & T outlays for several sectors in the Seventh Plan was not available, the relevant columns are left blank. *Included under Chemicals and fertilizers sector.

member Science Advisory Council. The Science Advisory Council advises the prime minister on (i) major issues facing science and technology today, (ii) the health of science and technology in the country and the direction in which it should move. The council consists of eleven distinguished scientists and industrialists and is serviced by the department of science and technology (DST).

There are several S & T departments dealing with specific areas of S & T. Many of these departments have R & D laboratories under them and some public-sector production undertakings. A full-fledged ministry of science and technology was created in 1985 encompassing three specific S & T departments. In order to accelerate the process of technological change in various socio-economic sectors, Science and Technology Advisory Committees (STAC) exist in various economic

Table 13.2   Science and technology indicators (data are for 1986 unless otherwise stated)

1. Number of research institutions including specialized laboratories	1,300
2. Private research associations/institutes/foundations/ centres	539
3. In-house R & D unit (public and private sectors) (1987)	1,015
4. Science academies	3
5. Universities	160
6. Number of consultancy firms	>150
7. Learned societies	>70
8. Total estimated personnel in R & D sector	2.410,000
9. Out-turn of S & T personnel (annual) (nos)	190,000
10. Enrolment of students at university level (million nos)	1.086
11. Number of research papers published per year	>20,000
12. Number of patents filed (1985–86)	3,593
13. S & T outlay (Rs. billion)	
Sixth plan (1980–5)	34
Seventh plan (1985–90)	76
14. S & T expenditure (Rs. billion)	
Sixth plan (1980–5)	64
Seventh plan (1985–8) (estimated)	84
15. S & T expenditure as percentage of GNP	1.10%
16. Rank among industrialized countries world-wide	27

ministries. An Inter-sectoral Science and Technology and Technology Advisory Committee serviced by the DST coordinates the work of STACs and looks into interdisciplinary problems cutting across the various economic sectors. As part of the evolving process of organization of science and technology several new departments were created during the sixth five-year plan (1980–5) to give thrust to emerging areas. These departments grew out of the programmes initiated by the DST during the earlier plan periods. The S & T activities in the educational system are mainly carried out through the 160 universities, the Institute of Science and the five Indian Institutes of Technology.

These organizations receive major financial support from the government through the allocation made by the Planning Commission which is responsible for preparing five-year development plans for the country. Allocation made to various sectors during the seventh plan period (1985–90) are shown in Tables 13.1(a) and 13.1(b). An analysis based on these figures indicates that about 55 per cent of the total S & T outlay for the seventh plan went to the scientific departments directly dealing with S & T activities (for example, atomic energy, space, ocean development, ministry of S & T, etc.) while the S & T component of the socio-economic ministries (for example health, agriculture, coal, communication, power, steel, etc.) accounted for about 45 per cent of the total allocation for S & T in the seventh plan (for details please see next section).

An analysis of the selected S & T indicators is summarized in Table 13.2[9] which gives an indication of the impact produced as a result of allocation to S & T activities over the successive five-year plans since the 1950s. A new mechanism for taking up inter-agency programmes which will have societal impact was introduced in the seventh plan (1985–90). These programmes called 'Technology Missions' cover the entire range of activities from R & D to actual delivery of products and services required for solving societal problems.[10]

INSTITUTIONAL INFRASTRUCTURE FOR RESEARCH

The R & D activities are carried out by institutions that come under Central and State government departments, industrial units, professional bodies, and by university-type structures.[11]

Research institutions under central government departments are generally grouped under councils or commissions to provide flexibility and autonomy. For example the Council of Scientific and Industrial Research with forty-two research institutions is a registered society with the prime minister as its president. Agricultural research institutions are grouped under the Indian Council of Agricultural Research; and similarly medical institutions are under the India Council of Medical Research. Such councils and commissions are headed by scientists and consist of outside experts, representatives of finance, ministries, industry and other users of research output. For several research institutions belonging to central government departments such councils or commission structures do not exist; instead, advisory committees oversee their research activities. There are 496 research institutions under central government departments (1988).

The state governments have also set up institutions primarily for meeting the R & D needs of traditional sectors like agriculture, animal husbandry, public health, forestry, etc. These institutions also engage in survey and extension activities. There are 178 institutions of this category (1988).

With the introduction of incentive schemes for research, a large number of public and private industries have set up in-house R & D centres (numbering 1,015 in 1987). These centres carry out research and development work to update technology, effect improvement in the manufacturing process, introduce new products/processes and develop substitutes for imported items. The investment on R & D as a percentage of sales turnover by the industrial sector as a whole has been of the order of 0.71 per cent (1987 figures).

Other categories of institutions that carry out R & D activities are associations of industries, research foundations set up by industrial houses or philanthropic organizations, voluntary groups and professional societies. These institutions can also receive funds from the government (in 1987 there were 1,085 such R & D institutions).

The universities provide trained manpower for research institutions and themselves carry out scientific research. The number of universities has grown from twenty in 1947 to 160 in 1987. Approximately 9 per cent of national R & D expenditure goes to the university system for research. Funds from the University Grants Commission received regularly by the universities are primarily used for teaching purposes, and project funding schemes of various government departments are the main sources for carrying out research at universities. Some of the government departments have set up units and common research facilities in universities to facilitate research in areas of their concern.

Universities in India produce around 3,500 doctorates every year in various branches of science, technology, engineering, medical and other fields (estimates of 1986). The total stock of science and technology manpower generated by the education system increased to 2.6 million in 1985 from a mere 0.2 million in 1950 and yet the number per thousand population in 1985 was only 3.43 and out of these only about 0.2 per thousand were employed in R & D.

THE PLANNING PROCESS

Since India adopted a planned approach for its development, planning for S & T also becomes part of the national planning exercise. The Planning Commission plays a central role in formulating the national S & T plan with the involvement of scientists, technologists and representatives of concerned agencies and departments. The five-year S & T plan has two broad components, reflecting the programmes on various organizational structures for S & T: the S & T activities of 'S & T Agencies' and the 'Socio-Economic Agencies' or the so-called economic ministries (please see Tables 13.1a and 13.1b). As stated earlier, in the 1985–90 plan period 55 per cent of the government allocation for S & T went to the S & T agencies and 45 per cent in relation to the S & T targets of the socio-economic agencies. Some of the S & T agencies themselves engage in industrial or production activities. Such programmes of S & T agencies are considered under the plans of individual socio-economic agencies. For example, the power generation plan of the department of atomic energy is considered along with the plans of the ministry of energy.

The preparation of the five-year S & T plan is an elaborate exercise. Once the overall approach to the main five-year plan has been articulated by the National Development Council, preparation of the sectoral plans is taken up. The responsibility for preparing the plan for the S & T sector is entrusted to the member of the Planning Commission in charge of S & T. The entire exercise involves extensive consultations with agencies, individual experts and non-governmental organizations (for example science academies). This exercise results in a chapter on S & T in the plan document.[7] This chapter identifies the main issues to be tackled by the S & T plan, the nature of programmes to be taken up by different S & T agencies either individually or collectively and an indicative distribution of financial resources. For example, for the eighth five-year plan (1990–5), fourteen task forces have been set up to examine issues such as basic research, mechanisms for transfer of technologies; the mission approach; application for S & T for basic needs, S & T-based employment; prioritization, etc. Elaborating upon the S & T chapter in the five-year-plan document, individual S & T agencies formulate their

Table 13.3   Total national expenditure on R & D

Financial year	Expenditure (in million Rs.)	Percentage of GNP
1948–9	11.00	0.18
1958–9	22.93	0.35
1968–9	1075.06	0.63
1978–9	5462.01	0.63
1987–8	30778.00	1.01

own five-year plans. These are submitted to the Planning Commission for discussions at the beginning of the five-year-plan period and subsequently on an annual basis.

The planning process takes into account the plans of the central government and also those of the twenty-five political states and seven union territories. During the sixth five-year plan (1980–5), state level S & T departments/agencies were set up to encourage preparation of S & T plans for the states. Almost all of the states and union territories in the country have structures for planning state-level S & T activities and these programmes are also discussed with the Planning Commission along with the overall state plans.

The national S & T plan and the agency plans constitute the framework for programme and project planning at the institution level. In operational terms the planning exercise starts simultaneously at the national and the institution level. Institutions make draft plans that are integrated by the parent agency as inputs to the national plan discussions. The composition of the working groups that prepare the national plan ensures that membership of the relevant agencies get inputs emerging from the institution-level exercises.

The financial allocation for the S & T sector is finalized by the member of the Planning Commission in charge of the S & T through a joint consultative process involving members of the Planning Commission representing other sectors such as industry, agriculture, education, etc. and the ministry of finance.

FINANCIAL RESOURCES FOR RESEARCH AND DEVELOPMENT

The total national expenditure on research and development is shown in Table 13.3.

The government is the main source of funds (of the order of 85–90 per cent of national S & T expenditure). The private sector accounts for only 10–11 per cent.[11]

Research institutions of the central government agencies are also the principal users of the national funds. For example, during the three-year period 1985–8, the ministry of defence accounted for 37 per cent, the department of space 17 per cent, the Council of Scientific and Industrial Research 11 per cent, the department of atomic energy 10 per cent, the

Table 13.4   Foreign collaborations, 1981–7

Country	1981	1982	1983	1984	1985	1986	1987	Total	%
USA	85	109	135	143	229	203	217	1121	21.2
FRG	74	110	129	132	187	188	154	974	18.4
UK	80	105	119	123	149	134	130	840	15.9
Japan	27	51	58	78	111	111	82	518	9.8
Italy	18	37	30	37	59	58	54	293	5.5
France	23	28	40	38	63	40	43	275	5.2
Switzerland	26	41	47	30	43	32	32	251	4.7
Sweden	11	15	15	14	32	30	20	137	2.6
Netherlands	9	13	13	14	18	24	30	114	2.2
Others	36	79	87	131	150	140	148	771	14.5
Total	389	588	673	740	1041	960	903	5294	100.0

Table 13.5   Foreign collaborations: by sector, 1981–7

Sector	Number	%
Alternate/renewable energy sources	35	0.7
Chemical	584	11.2
Electrical and electronics	1,288	24.7
Industrial machinery	986	18.9
Mechanical engineering	659	12.6
Machine tool	152	2.9
Metallurgy	259	5.0
Textile	62	1.2
Transport	247	4.7
R & D/consultancy	57	1.1
Miscellaneous	883	17.0
Total	5,212*	100.0

* Excludes 82 cases approved by administrative ministries, under delegated powers in 1981, whose sectoral breakdown is not available.

Indian Council of Agriculture 10 per cent and the remaining 15 per cent was shared by other S & T agencies and universities.[9]

INTERNATIONAL COLLABORATION

International collaboration is carried out through joint research projects and exchange of scientists and technology transactions. To facilitate these, bilateral S & T agreements exist with about forty countries. Special emphasis is placed on promoting cooperation among the developing countries. India has set aside 10 per cent of its indicative planning figure (IPF) for United Nations Development Programme (UNDP) for Technical Cooperation among Developing Countries (TCDC). India also participates in almost all programmes of the United Nations relating to science and technology.

Policies for bilateral technology transactions are formulated from time to time in conformity with the developmental plans. As can be seen from Table 13.4 the number of foreign collaborations has increased steadily since 1980. The sectoral distribution (Table 13.5) shows that the greatest number of collaborations are in the electrical and electronics sector.

CONCLUSION

Policies, strategies and structures for S & T have evolved in India under a planned development approach. The problem of meeting the basic needs of a large and growing population continues to dominate the planning process. The coupling of an extensive infrastructure for S & T with the administrative machinery for socio-economic development necessarily requires a process of accommodation; more so under the co-existence of public and private enterprises. The planning process has remained flexible, and concomitantly plans and programmes for S & T also show a degree of fluidity. Communication of perceptions between those involved in decisionmaking through committees and consultative bodies is an important integrating mechanism that is reflected in policy documents dealing with S & T. It is due to this interactive process of decisionmaking that strengths and weaknesses emerge and adjustments occur in plans and programmes.

Indian science is beginning to learn to develop in a much less protected environment. The 'import-substitution' phase is over, easy access to funds for research is no longer taken for granted and the need for tackling the entire innovation chain is being understood. A stage has come when the scientists and researchers are expanding their constituency to encompass actors engaged in production, service and commercial activities. Accommodation among this wider constituency will continue to change the planning process and institutional structures for science and technology in India.

NOTES

1. Constitution of India, Central Law Agency, Allahabad, 1984, p. 22.
2. Scientific Policy Resolution, Government of India, New Delhi, 4 March 1958.
3. Technology Policy Statement, Government of India, New Delhi, January 1983.
4. Industrial Policy Resolution, Government of India, New Delhi, 6 April 1948.
5. *An Approach to the Science and Technology Plan*, National Committee on Science and Technology, New Delhi, January 1973.
6. Science and Engineering Research Council, 1980–7, Department of Science and Technology, New Delhi, 1988.
7. The Sixth Five-Year Plan, 1980–5, Planning Commission, New Delhi, 1980; The Seventh Five-Year Plan, 1985–90, Planning Commission, New Delhi, 1985.
8. *Annual Report, 1987–88*, Department of Scientific and Industrial Research, New Delhi, 1988.
9. Science and Technology, Festival of India 1985–6, Department of Science and

Technology, New Delhi.
10. *Status Report on Science and Technology in India 1988*, Publication and Information Directorate, Council of Scientific and Industrial Research, New Delhi, 1988.
11. Research and Development Statistics — 1986–7, Department of Science and Technology, Government of India, New Delhi.

14 Science and technology policies in The Netherlands*

W. Hutter

NATIONAL CONTEXT OF SCIENCE AND TECHNOLOGY POLICY

The Netherlands is among the smaller countries in the OECD. Some 14.5 million people live in an area of only 41,500 square kilometres, which represents one of the highest population density figures in the world. Internationally The Netherlands has long been famous for its battle against the sea. This has led to a strong tradition in the field of civil engineering. Because of its geographical position, The Netherlands fulfils an important transit role in Western Europe. The Netherlands also has a highly developed agrarian sector and as a result it is among the largest exporters of agricultural products in the world.

In post-war economic development, priority was given to the creation and maintenance of human capital. Since the 1960s the exploitation of large energy reserves in the form of natural gas has played a particularly important role. At present the Dutch economy is undergoing a process of adaptation and recovery. Following a deep economic recession at the end of the 1970s, recent years have been characterized by an improvement in the economic situation. Dutch industrial structure is characterized by the presence of five large multinational concerns, the relatively large share held by processing and production of semi-manufactured goods, and energy-intensive processes and products. The figures in Table 14.1 will suffice to present the macroeconomic picture.

Scale and dynamics of R & D activity

The highly developed Dutch research system is diverse and covers virtually the entire spectrum of science and technology. Traditionally much attention is devoted to basic research.

Typically, the largest part (two-thirds) of R & D funded by the private sector is accounted for by five multinational concerns based in The Netherlands. The top laboratories of these multinationals thus have a significance for training and other research in The Netherlands which should not be underestimated. Compared with other countries, it can be said that a relatively large part of government-financed R & D is carried

* Prepared under the supervision of Dr W. Hutter, secretary of the Advisory Council for Science Policy in The Netherlands (RAWB) and partly adapted from the OECD report, *Reviews of National Science and Technology Policy*, the Hague, 1987.

Table 14.1   A number of key macroeconomic figures for 1986

Gross National Product	: 420 billion guilders (1986 prices)
Employment (× 1,000 work-years)	: 4.600

Distribution of employment among companies (× 1,000 work-years)
Agriculture	: 270
Industry	: 860
Energy	: 55
Construction	: 320
Services	: 2,370 (public service: 725)

Inflation	: −5‰
Gross investment ratio private sector	: 12% (in % GNP)
Unemployment	: 15.4% (in % labour force)
	725,000 persons

out within the technical-scientific infrastructure (universities and other research institutes). Within this infrastructure, however, The Netherlands has an exceptional research organization, in size as well as in scope, in The Netherlands Organization for Applied Scientific Research (TNO), (see Chapter 3). It is notable that the Dutch government has long opted for the promotion of technical-scientific, industrial and technological, and agricultural research by means of an adequate R & D infrastructure, rather than through direct funding of research by companies.

The distribution of R & D expenditure over the various sectors (industry, research institutes and universities) has been subject to gradual change only since the start of the 1970s. This also applies to the distribution of research expenditure. A number of shifts have taken place in state expenditure on research. The share of the agriculture and fisheries ministry has fallen from some 10 per cent (1973–8) to 6.8 per cent in 1985 and the share of the economic affairs ministry has risen from an average of some 10 per cent in the first half of the 1970s to 20.1 per cent in 1985. Expenditure on basic research (universities, para-university institutes) hovers around a more or less constant level of 55 per cent. In respect of funding of R & D efforts, it can be said that The Netherlands compared reasonably favourably on an international level until after 1978 when a number of industrialized nations increased their R & D efforts and The Netherlands threatened to fall behind. In the last few years some of the lost ground appears to have been regained through increased private-sector efforts in the R & D field (see also Chapter 4). Growth in R & D expenditure in industry in real terms has been 4–5 per cent per year for some time. Table 14.2 gives a comparative international survey of R & D expenditure by governments and the private sector.

At present the minister for education and science is responsible for the coordination of science policy. This cooperation is carried out on the basis of a model in which every minister is responsible for his policy, but policy proposals are correlated to the main points of the coordinatory policy in consultation with the coordinating minister. The minister for economic affairs is responsible for technology policy and thus also for inter-ministerial coordination in this field. He is particularly charged with

Table 14.2   Total expenditure and expenditure by Government and industry on R & D in the European Community member states, the United States and Japan, in per cent of Gross Domestic Product (GDP) in 1985

	Total	Government	Private sector
The Netherlands	2.1	1.0	1.0
FRG	2.6	1.1	1.5
France	2.3	1.2	1.0
Italy	1.3	0.6	0.6
Belgium	1.4	0.4	0.9
UK	2.3	1.1	0.9
Denmark	1.2	0.6	0.5
European Community	1.9	1.1	0.8
USA	2.8	1.4	1.3
Japan	2.8	0.8	1.7

industrially orientated research and with energy research. In addition, he is primarily responsible for TNO, maritime research and the fields of space research and space technology. The preparations for political decisionmaking at ministerial level on S & T policy are structured as follows. The so-called Council for Science and Technology Policy (RWT) functions as a subordinate council to the cabinet. Subordinate councils in The Netherlands are chaired by the prime minister and consist of the ministers most concerned in the relevant section of policy. The interdepartmental commissions for science policy and for technology policy function as the civil service back-up for the Council for Science and Technology policy.

Finally, it should be mentioned that a ministerial council for information policy has been set up, chaired by the prime minister, for which decisionmaking is prepared in the civil service by the interdepartmental commission for information policy. Table 14.3 contains a survey of the most important advisory bodies, intermediary agencies are covered in Table 14.4 and executive R & D organizations in the field of science and technology are surveyed in Table 14.5. Some more information about the spending on R & D is contained in Tables 14.6–14.9.

VOCATIONAL TRAINING, UNIVERSITY EDUCATION AND RESEARCH

Introduction

This section deals with organizations and institutions of research and education involved with industrial research that are the responsibility of the minister of education and science. This group of organizations and institutions includes nine universities, three technological universities, one 'open' university, seven teaching hospitals, more than forty research institutions, The Netherlands Organization for the Advancement of Science (NWO), The Royal Netherlands Academy of Arts and Sciences,

Table 14.3   Advisory bodies

Advisory body	Task	Minister primarily involved
Advisory Council for Science Policy (RAWB)	Advising on science and technology policy	Education and science Economic affairs
Royal Netherlands Academy of Arts and Sciences (KNAW)	Advising on scientific fields	Education and science
Advisory Council for Higher Education (ARHO)	Advising on education and research in universities	Education and science
Sector Councils:	Advising on research and development in social priority areas	
— National Council for Agricultural Research (NRLO)		Agriculture and fisheries
— Council for Environment and Nature Research (RMNO)		Housing, regional development & environment
— Advisory Council for Scientific Research in the framework of Development Aid (RAWOD)		Foreign affairs
— Programming platform for Regional Development Research (PRO)		Housing, regional development and environment
— Council for Health Research (RGO)		Welfare, health and culture
Ad hoc Exploration Committee (e.g. chemistry, biology, physics)	Advising on scientific fields	Education and science
Programming Committees (e.g. criminology, welfare research)	Advising on research budgets	Various

about 1,300 junior secondary vocational schools, about 550 senior secondary vocational schools and about 400 institutions for higher vocational training. In addition to this group there is one agricultural university and institutions for higher agricultural training under the minister of agriculture and fisheries. Both ministers coordinate their policies effectively so that higher agricultural training is an integrated part of the higher education system in The Netherlands. Recent developments in the institutional structure of this system will be discussed in the next section.

For education involving industrial research, there are three kinds of institutions in The Netherlands: (i) universities, (ii) institutions of vocational training and (iii) the Open University; all are almost entirely

Table 14.4   Intermediary agencies

Intermediary agencies (not exclusive)	main tasks	Minister primarily involved
Netherlands Organization for the Advancement of Science (NWO)	Funding of university/basic research	Education and science
Foundation for Technical Services (STW)	Funding of technical-scientific university research	Education and science
Foundation for Coordination of Maritime Research (SCMO)	Formulation of research programmes	Economic affairs
Foundation for Educational Research (SVO)		Education and science
Steering Committee for innovation directed Research Programmes (IOPs)		Economic affairs
National Institute for Aerospace (NIVR)		Economic affairs
Applied research for roads and waterways		Transport

financed by the government. To a large extent, each university is autonomous in the organization of its teaching and research activities. The relationships between universities and the government are to a large extent determined by negotiations about the allocation of funds between the executive boards of the universities and the minister. Of course, the agreed model of allocation of funds and the total amount of funds available cannot be affected by these negotiations.

The vocational system provides vocational training on three different levels, each providing a theoretical and practical preparation for specific professions. The junior secondary vocational training lasts for at most four years and has direct entry from primary school. Entry to *higher vocational training* is open to secondary-school leavers. The system of higher vocational training is considerably more fragmented than the university system; in 1982, the number of students per college varied between 100 and 6,000. The Open University became operational in September 1984 as an independent institution of open higher education; it consists of a central establishment in Heerlen and eighteen study centres throughout The Netherlands.

As far as research is concerned, the Open University and the higher vocational institutes are of minor importance: institutes of higher vocational training have research activities only in arts and in some applications. It is the policy of the minister of education and science, however, that these research activities should be supported. All three levels of

Table 14.5 Executive R & D organizations

R & D organizations (not exclusive)	research field	personnel 1987 (full-time equivalents)	budget/ year 1985 (m. Dutch guilders)	Minister primarily involved
The Netherlands Organization for Applied Scientific Research (TNO)	industrial-technological, defence, health, food, technology and society	4,050	606	Education and science
Universities and technical universities	basic research	15,000	2,000	Education and science and agriculture and fisheries
Large-scale technical-scientific institutions:				
— Netherlands Centre for Energy Research (ECN)	energy research	870	130	Economic affairs
— Laboratory for Soil Mechanics (LGM)	soil-mechanical and foundation technology	280	35	Transport
— Maritime Research Institute Netherlands (MARIN)	shipbuilding, ocean-engineering	320	37	Economic affairs
— Hydraulics Laboratory (WL)	watercourse, water transportation, industrial liquid transport	555	70	Transport
— National Aviation and Space Laboratory (NLR)	aviation and aerospace technology	826	107	Transport
Agricultural Institutes (research institutions, testing institutions)	agriculture, forestry, fisheries	3,450	333	Agriculture and fisheries
Institutions managed by KNAW (Royal Netherlands Academy for Arts and Sciences)	among others: brain research, embryological research, ecological research	535	52	Education and science
Institutions managed by NWO (see Table 14.2)	mathematics, information technology	1,240	131	Education and science
State Institute for Health and Environmental Protection (RIVM)	public health, environmental	1,215	120	Welfare, health and culture

Table 14.6   Changes in total research spending, by sectors (in millions of guilders and as a percentage of GNP)

	1980		1986		1987		1988	
	m. gld.	% GNP	m. gld.	% GNP	m. gld.	% GNP	m. gld.	% GNP
Central Government, of which	3654	1.09	4093	0.95	4292	0.99	4188	0.96
— universities	1706	0.51	1690	0.39	1700	0.39	1630	0.37
— other institutes	1948	0.58	2413	0.56	2592	0.60	2558	0.59
Private sector	2964	0.88	4400	1.03	4550	1.05	4700	1.07
Other	499	0.15	460	0.11	460	0.11	460	0.10
Total	7177	2.12	8953	2.09	9302	2.15	9348	2.13
GNP (market prices, billions of guilders)	335.8		429.2		432.05		438.16	

Table 14.7   1987 budget figures and 1992 estimates for all research funding, classified according to areas of government responsibility (in percentages)

	final budget 1987	estimates 1992
1. Environment (exploration, etc.)	0.6	0.6
2. Infrastructure and planning policy	4.5	4.5
3. Environmental pollution	3.4	3.3
4. Health research	2.4	2.5
5. Energy	3.6	4.1
6. Agriculture	4.1	4.1
7. Industrial productivity and technology	18.8	14.8
8. Social structures and relationships	2.4	2.4
9. Space research	3.3	3.6
10. University research	39.6	40.7
11. Non-application-oriented research	10.1	11.8
12. Miscellaneous research	4.2	4.2
13. Defence	2.7	3.1
Total	100 = 4.292 m. gld.	100 = 4.144 m. gld.

vocational training are of growing importance within the framework of science and technology policy.

Some recent developments in the system of higher education

University research
The minister of education and science has an important policy instrument at his disposal for university research in the form of organization and

Table 14.8 R & D spending (actual) as a percentage of GNP; comparisons with the European Community, USSR, USA and Japan

	1972	1974	1976	1978*	1980	1981	1982	1983	1984	1985
USSR	3.71	3.74	3.61	3.54	3.76	3.75	3.68			
USA	2.52	2.40	2.37	2.32	2.46	2.51	2.66	2.72	2.74	2.88
Japan	1.94	2.02	2.00	2.00	2.22	2.32	2.42	2.56	2.65	
Europe (the 10)			1.81	1.87	1.89	1.99	2.03	2.05		
FRG	2.21	2.13	2.16	2.25	2.42	2.45	2.58	2.54		
UK†	2.06	2.03	2.06	2.09	2.31	2.42	2.34	2.28		
France	1.86	1.80	1.77	1.76	1.84	2.01	2.10	2.15	2.22	2.27
Italy	0.91	0.83	0.86	0.84	0.86	1.01	1.04	1.12	1.25	1.27
Netherlands	2.05	1.94	1.97	1.87	1.89	1.88	1.97	2.03	1.99	2.00
Belgium	1.40	1.37	1.34	1.40	1.42	1.47	1.43	1.46		
Denmark	0.97	0.96	0.96	0.96	1.03	1.10	1.13	1.10		
India									0.96	

Source: OECD

* The Netherlands' GNP was revised upwards in 1979, which results in a break in the trend
† Sciences

financing of the universities. This policy instrument includes the following aspects:

(i)   the universities are to be able to act as autonomous bodies,
(ii) the research plans of the universities are to take into account national discipline-by-discipline recommendations and
(iii) a substantial part of the research projects at universities is to be financed by a national research organization (NWO) which, unlike the universities, need not consider teaching aspects.

Consequently, the research activities are funded through a system of 'multiple financing': for funding, researchers may apply to different sources with different decisionmaking procedures.

The *first* source of funding comes directly from the minister of education and science. The universities receive these funds as a part of their total budget. Critical surveys by the RAWB (1971) and the OECD examiners (1973) concluded that the government (and society) were insufficiently informed about the allocation of these funds and their effects: the funds were merely distributed by means of a formula related to the number of students at each university. As a drop in student numbers is expected for the late 1980s a model has been introduced in which the allocation of grants is not entirely dependent on the number of students: the *Plaatsen-Geld-Model*. In this model, the funds are still distributed among the universities as a lump sum, but now this sum is calculated from four components: three A-components, for which annual reporting on the use of funds is sufficient, and one B-component which consists of conditionally financed research programmes (*Voorwaardelijke Financiering*). These programmes are to be protected from budgetary cuts by both the universities and the minister of education and science. After five years, continuation of funding for conditionally financed programmes depends on the proper use of funds for the purposes agreed; this may lead to changes in the lump sums that are currently received by the universities.

The second source of funding is also granted by the government, but allocated to the universities through independent organizations such as NWO and STW (Foundation for Technical Science). NWO is the most important; its foundations and study groups play a major role in the coordination of university research. Basic points in this arrangement are that (i) the funding system should be controlled by the scientists themselves and that (ii) scientific research should not be dissociated from the universities. About half of NWO's total budget is used to finance projects in university research through this second source. A large proportion of these projects lasts for three or four years and involves PhD students. Most projects are based on proposals which have been positively vetted by independent (expert) review. Also NWO itself may take the initiative to finance a particular project.

The third source of funding is derived from a miscellaneous collection of financial sources: private foundations, government agencies, companies, etc. Usually, the purpose of research projects funded by these sources is to solve concrete problems for anyone willing to pay for this service, and are generally referred to as 'contract research' projects. By carrying out contract research, the research capacity of a university can be increased, and the university scientist becomes better informed on problems in society.

The relation between government and university research

In the near future, two kinds of documents will occupy a central place in university planning: the development plans of the individual universities and the higher education and university research plan ('HOOP') of the government. In their development plans the universities submit their plans and aspirations and are subject to judgements from advisory bodies relevant to the universities' activities and to previous higher education plans. The HOOP-plan, on the other hand, contains the government's medium-term plans for the system of higher education and university research, and is based on developing plans of universities.

SCIENCE POLICY

Scope and responsibilities

The position and significance of Dutch science policy can best be illustrated by a sketch of the developments which have taken place over the last ten to fifteen years. Following the first moves towards coordination of science policy in the 1960s, this area of policy became a political issue at the start of the 1970s. Political recognition then took shape in the form of a minister-without-portfolio charged with coordination of science policy.

In the early 1970s awareness of the social significance of science and technology developed at a political level. Social issues became more complex, and the intermingling of sectors more manifest. In science and technology interdisciplinary boundaries faded. Furthermore, during this period it was realized that the explosive growth which the research system had experienced in the 1950s and 1960s could not continue *ad infinitum*. It was against this background that the need for a more open research system and a more explicit science policy was recognized.

A first milestone was the science policy Memorandum (1974) which listed the following as the main aims of science policy: improving the quality and effectiveness of research, more orientation towards external requirements (opening the research system) and democratization in research. The administrative model selected was the concerted action model.

On the basis of these principles, science policy was, in the second half to the 1970s, strongly aimed at the aspect of process; in order to strengthen research coordination and cooperation, research programming was launched (for example in the form of national programmes in the energy and environment fields among others), concepts were developed for reinforcing external influences on research and research programming (The Sector Councils Memorandum, 1977) and the first moves towards reorganization of TNO were made in order to place this organization under more professional management.

At the end of the 1970s Dutch science policy took an important turn. Social questions such as unemployment, shortages (energy, — this problem had become manifest earlier — environment, physical planning) and problems relating to socio-cultural developments became urgent issues. On the level of science and technology, developments took place (micro-electronics, biotechnology, information technology) which had far-reaching effects on the entire society. This led to the conclusion that a more active government policy was required. A clear token was the publication of the Innovation Memorandum, which heralded a period of more specific promotion of science and technology. The Innovation Memorandum itself was aimed at the promotion of technological modernization in Dutch society, as well as general institutional measures and measures creating advantageous conditions (reductions in the costs of R & D for industry and promotion of information transfer); plans were presented for a functional promotion of research by means of government promotion funds, for example, Innovation-Orientated Research Programmes (IOPs).

During the same period, steps were taken to 'open out' university research. Such research became an independent policy object, in which quality in particular, but also social orientation, became criteria for the reinforcement of research programming and the protection of high-level university research (for the concept of conditional funding; see Chapter 2). Also in this period the reorganization of TNO entered an accelerated stage. After 1980 TNO was converted into a professionally led organization, far more responsive to scientific and technological challenges and external questions.

These changes in the late 1970s strongly affected science policy in the 1980s. In cooperation with other relevant ministries an active policy of research stimulation was pursued in the early 1980s, in a number of important fields such as micro-electronics, behavioural and social sciences, information services, biotechnology and space research. To a certain extent the removal to the ministry of economic affairs of tasks in the field of technology policy, particularly for the market sector, in the cabinet formation of 1982 also placed a different emphasis on science policy; the role of science policy now lies primarily in long-term research and in the multi-faceted integrated-system conceptions (e.g., satellite observations, telecommunications, transport). In the field of earth-observation this implies, for example, an integrated approach to space- and groundbased systems, as well as data processing.

The research-system: outline of the current position

The R & D system in The Netherlands financed by the government comprises, in addition to the universities (see Chapter 2), a relatively extensive system of non-university research institutes. In these research institutes the emphasis lies primarily on strategic and applied research, particularly in the physical, agricultural and technical sciences, with a view to application. In these fields the universities concentrate on basic and strategic research. However, applied research, often on commission, in the fields of the social and medical sciences does take place to a large extent in the universities as well.

Multi-faceted

Non-university research, carried out in some 140 institutes, is remarkable for its multi-faceted nature.

— While many institutes are independent, others form part of a larger system (for example, TNO, NWO, KNAW).
— The structure of institutional organizations varies widely: TNO is a centrally managed organization with a divisional structure, whereas NWO, for instance, offers far more of a federated relationship.
— Many institutes and organizations have been incorporated into one department, while others, (for example TNO) maintain financial and administrative relationships with more than one department.
— The financial and administrative relationships between institutes and organizations and with departments differ: whereas TNO and NWO hold an autonomous position, the agricultural research institutes (DLO) were until recently strictly controlled by the ministry of agriculture and fisheries.
— The procedures for setting up research programmes and the financial relationships with (potential) clients in government, industry and social organizations vary significantly.
— The legal status of staff in the institutes and organizations forms a patchwork: government civil servants are to be found in some, while other institutes have their own individual legal status regulations.

With regard to relationships among the institutes themselves, and between these institutes and the universities, there is to be found, beside intensive forms of cooperation, a wide-ranging diversification of research activities (for example in the field of environmental research) and even, in some cases, of mutual competition.

The institutional set-up has been confronted with a number of changes currently:

— Important changes are taking place in the 'markets', as a result of changing research requirements (for example in the public works sector or in health research) through the introduction of new technologies, and through a new intermingling of problem areas (for example environment with agriculture, energy and water management respectively). The clear tendency towards an increase in the expertise available at the institutes goes hand in hand with new forms of cooperation and new coordinatory questions.
— Changes in the international research context. The European dimension especially has been gaining much ground recently. The Dutch research potential will have to be linked to important scientific developments on the international level.

The research system: policy

General policy objectives
To an increasing degree the developments sketched above determined the policy concerning the research system. The general objectives are:

— promoting quality standards, on an international basis;
— reinforcing orientation towards external questions in the medium and long-term perspective;
— increasing coordination, cooperation and distribution of tasks in the research system;
— promoting efficient and effective operations in research institutes; attaining the best possible financial structure, investment policy, staffing policy and management.

An essential angle here is the introduction of 'non-intervention' administration: the government creates the conditions by which institutes and organizations are primarily responsible for their own strategic policy, although that policy may also be influenced by external consultations and by the formation of research programmes on a national scale, partly financed by extra funds.

Priorities in research
In the context of science policy, a system of priorities is gradually developing. One of the first effects of this can be found in recent science budgets. These expressly incorporate recommendations from temporary and permanent intermediary and advisory bodies. Direct government influence and the place of intermediary and advisory bodies and surveys are considered below.

Direct influence on the orientation of research is based on targeted promotion policy through government-launched promotion programmes on a national level. Intermediary and advisory bodies contribute to the preparation and implementation of research priorities which lead to the establishment of such programmes. Such organizations offer scope for more indirect forms of influence on research. Intermediary organizations promote the coordination, correlation and programming of research in specific fields.

The advisory structure still receives special attention. The Advisory Council for Science Policy (RAWB) has a general advisory function. This Council was created in 1966. Its members are prominent scientists, industrialists and trade-union officials. The Council advises, on request or on its own initiative, the Dutch government in the field of science policy in a national and international context. Each year the Council publishes its annual advice, which is partly a reaction to the annual science budget. In 1975 the sector councils concept was introduced: tripartite consultation and advice bodies (research, users, government) which set out the main points of research in social priority areas from a long-term perspective. Not only do sector councils and related organizations supply the main lines for research, they can also enter into direct contact with the research world and have a direct influence on the policy of the relevant organizations. The sector councils do not possess their own financial resources, but for interesting research projects they may call on the funds of the coordinating minister for science policy.

Technology assessment

Furthermore, the policy with regard to 'interaction of science and technology in society' (IWTS) should be pointed out: it is formulated by science policy in its coordinating function, in cooperation with the ministry of economic affairs. The main elements of the programme which is being initiated in this field are: technology assessment research and awareness stimulation as well as information about developments and consequences of science and technology. A sum of almost 28 million guilders has been made available for this programme for the next five years.

Science policy promotion programmes

Recently so-called 'spearhead' programmes have been developed, as part of a coordinating research policy, in close collaboration with departments, research institutions, social groups and organizations and the private sector. These programmes are designed to stimulate research activities in carefully selected fields. Criteria are: scientific and/or social interest, giving structure to the research effort. Science policy promotion is by definition of a temporary nature: once the promotion is terminated the activities are expected to have become integrated in existing frameworks.

Some of the present 'spearheads' of science policy are:

1. *Labour*
   The labour programme is attuned to the systematic refining of knowledge, given the far-reaching influence scientific progress has on labour as one of the production factors, and to the planning of the research effort in this field with five central themes (technology, labour and organization; labour and health; the labour market; social security).
2. *Health research*
   The health-research programme is aimed at a strengthening of university medical-biological toplevel research (25 million guilders for a period of 5 years) and at the innovation and reorientation of health research (patient-linked research in a number of fields such as rheumatism, chronic specific respiratory diseases, psychiatric diseases, the relation between environmental and behavioural factors and health (40 million guilders for five years)).
3. *Soil Protection*
   The soil-protection programme, which was launched in 1986, will be directed at the concentration and enlargement of fundamental knowledge about soil, the effects of pollution — cleaning up and prevention.

4. *Earth/observation*

To explore and exploit natural resources involving a number of government tasks and private-sector activities, high-quality information is indispensable. Against this background and in close consultation with those who are involved, a promotion programme for remote sensing has been developed.

5. Research into the effects of public-sector programmes: *programme-evaluation*

Certain fields of public-sector activities require profound decisions, in which a balance has to be struck with regard to the quality of services and financing possibilities. Knowledge of the consequences of such decisions is called for.

International cooperation

Clearly, for a country such as The Netherlands, which accounts for some 1 per cent of the world effort in the fields of R & D, international cooperation is of great importance. The considerations on which international scientific cooperation is based include the following:

— the intrinsically international character of research in certain fields (marine, climatological, environmental research);
— efficiency: international distribution of tasks and coordination;
— necessary collation of expertise (in advanced, complex programmes and projects);
— the size of the investment resources necessary for large-scale projects (for example high-energy physics, space research, nuclear fusion);
— the multinational scale of markets and manpower required in order to develop (commercially) new technologies;
— the stimulants to quality in research efforts which result from contacts with top-level international research; the international cooperation necessary to regain lost ground in certain areas.

International scientific cooperation, particularly on a European scale, has now acquired even greater priority for The Netherlands as a result of rapid developments in the field of science and technology and the strong competitive positions of Japan and the United States. On the basis of the above-mentioned considerations The Netherlands takes part in the following multilateral organizations (among others): the European Community (the context programme and special programmes), the United Nations, the European Space Agency; and in the field of basic research through CERN, ESO, EMBL, ESF and also through the ESA's scientific programmes.

To an increasing degree opportunities for cooperation in smaller-scale relationships, in which various skills and potentials complement each other in a meaningful way, are systematically being sought. Some examples are: the oceanographic Snellius II expedition (with Indonesia) Antarctic research (with West Germany) ANS, IRAS, SAX (astronomical satellites with the United Kingdom, the United States and Italy).

TECHNOLOGY POLICY

Scope and responsibilities

The aim of the market-orientated technology policy is to promote development and application of technological innovation in the market sector, to promote better orientation of the technological infrastructure (universities and research institutes) towards the needs of industry and intensification of the ties between research, education and the market sector. In other words, technology policy aims to contribute to the improvement of competitiveness of The Netherlands' market sector, both by creating optimal conditions for this, and through active stimulation. It is a necessary, but not a sufficient condition for improvement of the competitive strength of the Dutch industrial and service sector. The Netherlands' government believes that in order for the technology policy to succeed, it is of crucial importance that the market sector itself makes a significant effort by taking greater risks than it has done in the past. This is expressed by the efforts made in research and development of high-tech industry and services.

Technology policy and the private sector

Technology policy aimed at the intensification of the technological and innovating activities of the market sector can be divided into:

(a) a general promotion policy, to benefit all companies in the market sector in principle; and
(b) a more specific promotion policy, in which concrete priorities are set: for example the support of industrial R & D programmes, for instance by means of supporting feasibility studies in technologically promising areas.

The three most important financial tools in this context are the following. For the purpose of general ('generic') promotion policy, The Netherlands has the Innovation Stimulation Scheme (INSTIR) for which 220 million is allocated annually as well as the Technical Development Loan, for which 176 million has been allocated in 1985. For the purposes of the specific promotion policy 78 million has been available in 1985, as well as 67 million for activities involving the technical-scientific infrastructure.

General 'generic' policy

The 'generic' technology and innovation policy, which is directed at stimulation and modernization of products, processes and services in the market sector, concentrates on the high costs and risks involved in R & D activities. In order to restrict these high costs, The Netherlands decided in 1984 to implement the Innovation Stimulation Scheme for a period of five years. Under the terms of this scheme companies may apply for subsidization of wage costs for R & D work carried out by themselves or contracted out. The aim is to create the most favourable circumstances possible for innovation especially by small- and medium-sized firms and for carrying out the necessary R & D work.

The second tool available for the purpose of the 'generic' stimulation policy is the Technical Development Loan, which has been in effect since 1953. Under the terms of this scheme, companies may apply for a soft loan up to a maximum of 60 per cent of the development costs for promising products, in order to partially cover the high risks. If the product is commercially successful, loans must be repaid.

Specific policy with regard to the market sector
Specific policy means a stimulation of promising activities with a coherent approach to research, information, education and training. This approach necessarily includes a certain selectivity to avoid unnecessary diffusion of government means and thus to innovate industry in a structural manner. There is, however, no 'blueprint' approach and the responsibility of industry itself is still paramount.

In the view of The Netherlands' government the industrial innovation policy should gradually gain a more programme-orientated character. This programme-orientation involves a more aggressive and innovation-orientated industrial policy, including more attention to technological change in industry. With the programme approach experience has been gained in energy research, the Innovation Orientated Research Programmes and information technology research. Regarding these examples the following phases or steps can be distinguished:

— selection, by or in close consultation with industry, of promising technologies and product market combinations;
— pre-studies;
— setting up of research programmes for more than one year, including financial aspects, which are aimed at fostering the technological infrastructure, education and training, (inter)national transfer of knowledge, research programmes, etc.;
— publication of the above plans to initiate further proposals from industry.

The implementation of the specific policies should be flexible and informal with an involvement of industry in all programmed phases.

Technology policy and the public sector

Among the tasks assigned to the minister of economic affairs in the field of technology policy is that of interdepartmental coordination. In the context of this coordinating task, an inter-departmental network has emerged for the purpose of integrating technology policy into the policy fields of other departments. This has led to the allocation of more funds for technological development from other departments, and an increase in activities undertaken jointly with other departments.

It is also increasingly recognized in this respect that the government exerts a major influence on technological development, for instance by performing its regulatory function or as a purchaser of high-tech goods and services. Conversely, technology can be an excellent aid to fulfilling the tasks which the government sees as its duty in the various fields of state care (energy, environment, etc.).

With respect to purchasing The Netherlands' government has attempted for a number of years, within the boundaries set by EEC and GATT rules, to pursue an innovative policy aimed at elucidating the government market and improving procurement management procedures. The first task of the ministry of economic affairs is that of intermediary between purchasing ministries and future suppliers. Discussion with purchasing departments serves to gather information about future acquisition at an early phase in order to pave the way for product innovation.

As government expenditure in the field of information technology plays a prominent role in the entire acquisition policy, the government has established an external commission to advise on policy in this sector, resulting in a report, the main recommendations of which were endorsed by The Netherlands' government in the fall of 1985. These comprised a restructuring of the coordination of the government policy on information services, the stimulation of advanced government information services' projects, setting goals for data communication and the creation of greater transparency of the government market in order to raise the cooperation with industry to a higher level.

Technical-scientific infrastructure

Technical-scientific infrastructure includes universities and institutes of higher education in their entirety as well as non-university research institutes, including the so-called 'Large Technological Institutes' and dozens of smaller research institutes which are partly financed by the government. The government spends more than 2 billion a year on technological research carried out in the technical-scientific infrastructure by means of basic and special-purpose subsidies as well as by contract research.

Technology policy is aimed at improving the correlation between activities conducted within the technical-scientific infrastructure and the needs of the market sector. On the one hand this is done by increasing the importance of knowledge generated in the technical-scientific infrastructure, and on the other by improving the accessibility of universities and research institutes for the market sector, particularly for medium-sized and small firms. This involves policy aimed at strategic and applied research, as distinct from basic research, which is also carried out within the technical-scientific infrastructure but is of an entirely different nature (see Chapter 2). Increasingly TNO appears to be in a position to attract contract work from the private sector, the market. In 1983 this already accounted for 30 per cent of all TNO revenues, and in 1985 for 36 per cent. This enables TNO to more than compensate for a relative decline in state revenues.

The Netherlands' government employs the same principles in designing new financial and administrative relationships between the government and the so-called 'Large Technological Institutes' (GTIs). These are:

— Netherlands' Centre for Energy Research;
— Laboratory for Soil Mechanics;
— Hydraulics Laboratory;
— National Aviation and Space Laboratory;
— Maritime Research Institute Netherlands.

The GTIs form the link between basic Netherlands' scientific knowledge and practical technological application. In the context of technology policy efforts are made to maintain scientific knowledge at a high level in key technological areas, and, as with TNO, to bring about a better correlation with the requirements of the users, particularly industry.

An important instrument aimed at creating closer ties between the market sector and the technological infrastructure is the Innovation-Orientated Research Programmes (IOPs) which were established in 1981. This instrument is intended to (re)direct a significant part of the research which is currently carried out by institutes partly financed by the Government, in consultation between researchers and users, towards fields and themes which are important in the medium term for society, and in particular of the market sector. The focus of these Innovation-Orientated Research Programmes is on university research, but the GTIs as well as other non-university research institutes are also involved.

The essence of the IOPs is that users, in particular companies, support the significance of the relevant field of research and help to draw up the programme, partly by participating in the programme commissions formed for each programme.

The original IOPs were: biotechnology, construction, equipment for the handicapped, and membranes-technology. Recently three new IOPs have been added: polymer-composites and special polymers; technical ceramics and carbohydrates. Furthermore plans have been made for setting up an IOP on Very Large Scale Integration in the microelectronics area. Also in the areas of catalysis and opto-electronics preparations are made to start IOPs. Experience gained with IOPs shows a need for further rules regarding industrial and intellectual property. A model contract between state, programme-management and research institutes contributes to better arrangements in this area. The IOP budget for 1986 amounted to 30 million.

International aspects of technology policy

A small country like The Netherlands with an open and internally-orientated economy allows its technology policy to depend on international technological developments to a large degree. International cooperation and exchange of information is thus regarded as essential by The Netherlands, on a multilateral as well as bilateral level.

On a multilateral level The Netherlands gives priority to cooperation within the European Community and more recently to EUREKA. In recent years The Netherlands has shown itself a strong supporter of shifts in emphasis within the European Community toward activities in the field of R & D and has called for more industry-orientated programmes and more market orientation in the Community research institutes. Other forms of multilateral cooperation which are highly valued by The Netherlands are OECD and COST.

In addition to these forms of multilateral cooperation, bilateral cooperation with a number of countries has been initiated.

Appendix I Opening remarks: Some observations on the Indian science and technology scene

Vasant Gowariker

In the present-day world, science and technology are intimately linked with social welfare, and the advancement of the two is symbiotic. The realization of a nation's aspirations, its prosperity and indeed the overall progress of a country is dependent on the advancement of science and technology in that country.

One of the dominating features of the contemporary world is the cultivation of science and technology on a large scale. For the first time in history, this activity has given the common man in advanced countries a standard of living and facilities and amenities which were once the preserve of an elite few in the population. Of this, The Netherlands provides as good an example as any, despite its small size.

In India, while we have a long way to go to accomplish, for a vast majority of our people, what a country like The Netherlands has already achieved, our commitment and determination to harness science for our people is clear and unequivocal. The government of India's Scientific Policy Resolution, passed by our Parliament in March 1958, states that commitment quite clearly. I will only quote a few lines to convey its essence.

The key to national prosperity, apart from the spirit of the people, lies, in the modern age, in the effective combination of three factors, technology, raw materials and capital, of which the first is perhaps the most important . . . it is an inherent obligation of a great country like India, with its traditions of scholarship and original thinking and its great cultural heritage, to participate fully in the march of science, which is probably mankind's greatest enterprise today.

The Government of India have accordingly decided that the aims of their scientific policy will be —

to foster, promote, and sustain, by all appropriate means, the cultivation of science, and scientific research in all its aspects — pure, applied, and educational

to ensure an adequate supply, within the country, of research scientists of the highest quality, and to recognise their work as an important component of the strength of the nation . . .

and, in general, to secure for the people of the country all the benefits that can accrue from the acquisition and application of scientific knowledge.

There are other policy pronouncements in different forms issued by the government from time to time, but the Scientific Policy Resolution is perhaps the only document which clearly emphasizes the country's resolve regarding the pursuit of science and technology.

Our Scientific Policy Resolution has been backed by a political commitment to science and technology (S & T) at the highest level, and national commitment in terms of resources devoted to our S & T efforts. Investments in S & T have been increasing with every successive five-year plan: this investment was of the order of Rs.20 crores in the first plan and Rs.67 crores in the second, but is now Rs.7,535 crores in the current seventh plan period, 1985–90. The rising trend is likely to continue. Our total R & D expenditure, as a percentage of GNP, reached 1 per cent in 1986–7, as against 2–3 per cent being spent by some of the advanced countries like the United States, Japan and even higher figures for the Soviet Union and some other European countries.

As a result of our efforts, we have built up quite a bit of infrastructure, generated a good pool of our own scientific and technical manpower for work in a whole range of S & T areas, and set up numerous scientific, research and industrial establishments and institutions, during the past forty years following independence.

Among our many achievements, the attainment of self-sufficiency in food has been particularly satisfying. We have been able not only to do away with imports of food, but also build buffer stocks which have sustained the country through a number of drought years. We have many other notable successes in a number of areas, including those in high-tech areas like atomic energy and space. I don't know if it is a good or bad reflection on our policy and planning systems, but it is a fact that Indian scientists, engineers, technologists and doctors can be found holding top positions round the world.

India's accomplishments in the last forty years are by no means insignificant by any standards. However, in our own eyes, they are all dwarfed by the continuing problems of poverty, illiteracy and health being faced by a large majority of our common people, particularly those living in our rural areas. Our S & T achievements have not been able to benefit them as much as we would have liked them to. So this is an area which has now been chosen for particular attention.

The government of India, some time ago, launched six National Technology Missions for the accomplishment of specific tasks in a short period. These are:

(i)   Vaccination and immunisation of vulnerable population, especially children;
(ii) Edible oil seeds — intensive cultivation and oil manufacture;
(iii) Better communications
(iv) Drinking water in every village and water management;
(v)   National literacy mission; and
(vi) Technology mission on dairy development.

In all these, an attempt has been made to specify goals and targets clearly to be achieved within a specified time-frame. Accomplishment of each Mission will require active participation and cooperation of a large number of central and state-level agencies and organizations, including those from the voluntary sector. These missions pose challenges not only to the S & T community but also to our planners and managers and afford us an opportunity to begin integrating S & T into all aspects of our day-to-day living.

In addition to the above missions, a number of projects have been taken up in a mission mode. I will give only a few typical examples. One of the projects relates to the setting up of a National Centre for Medium Range Weather Forecasting (NCMRWF), to provide timely weather forecasts as part of agro-meteorological services to our farmers. The NCMRWF will have a country-wide inter-linked network of agro-met centres to disseminate to our farmers agricultural operation-related weather information.

For better management and utilization of our natural resources, a major satellite-based project has been launched with a view to establishing a National Natural Resources Management System (NNRMS) using remote sensing technology; a major adjunct to this system is the Natural Resources Data Management System (NRDMS) under which a computer-based methodology has been developed for storage, analysis and retrieval of data at different levels; a network of data bases covering all geographical districts is envisaged to help realize the goal of decentralized socio-economic planning.

It has been becoming increasingly obvious that we must forge stronger linkages and bonds between S & T needs of various sectors of our economy and research work going on in our S & T and R & D institutions. Towards this, among other things, we have recently set up Science & Technology Advisory Committees (STACs) for almost all economic ministries, along with an inter-sectoral STAC. This is an attempt not only to identify and address S & T input needs of a given sector, but also to examine the application potential of existing S & T developments in one sector for possible harnessing in another sector.

We are also in the process of putting together a mechanism to focus on technology information, forecasting and assessment. In due course, we expect this mechanism to help us in tackling matters and taking decisions relating to the choice of technologies in different sectors and their development, acquisition, introduction, promotion and marketing. Recently, for this purpose, the government of India have set up a Technology Information, Forecasting and Assessment Council (TIFAC) in the department of science and technology. TIFAC will obviously receive many inputs from the STACs that were mentioned earlier. We would like to know about and learn from the Dutch system of addressing such technology-related issues.

Our recent efforts also include initiation of major national programmes relating to the popularization of science and stimulation and spread of a 'scientific temper' among our people through a National Council for Science and Technology Communication in the department of science and technology which also help in the promotion of environmental awareness among the people through special campaigns. Promotion of entrepreneurship to mitigate unemployment and under-employment among science and technology graduates is being attempted through a National Science and Technology Entrepreneurship Development Board, also set up in the department of science and technology.

I have gone through some of your science policy documents. Your policy has no doubt been formulated according to your own specific needs. Whereas we would very much like to benefit from experience of others, we are quite clear that each country has to find its own solutions to its peculiar problems and that no ready-made recipes would be able to fill the bill. This has accordingly been our approach to formulating our policies for the growth of science and technology in our country. Nevertheless, I am sure, both sides will be able to benefit from exchange of information, ideas and experiences in this area.

Appendix II Closing remarks

E. van Spiegel

With pleasure I take the opportunity to speak a few words at this dinner, just after closing our successful workshop on science and technology. When I left my country on Saturday afternoon, I was looking forward with great curiosity to the days to come. Indeed I was very interested to know how the idea of a workshop would develop in which experiences in the practice of science policy in our two countries would be compared.

For several reasons it took a few years to implement the idea of the workshop. I have to admit this slight delay has been most welcome to me because it has in fact given me time to adjust to my new role of co-chairman of the Joint Committee of Science and Technology. Also I had time to become more familiar with developments in the field of science and technology in India.

However, there is a second reason why this particular timing of the workshop suits me. The last year and a half we, at the department of science policy, have struggled through a process in which we tried to get a hold of what we experienced to be important new developments in and around the field of science policy. The main issues that came out of this struggle more or less coincide with the aspects that were discussed during our workshop.

Our first issue is:

— the increasing complexity of scientific problems and methods, of society and of decisionmaking processes;

The second one:

— shifting boundaries from public to private organizational structures in science and technology;

and the third one:

— a strong internationalization of science and technology along new, non-traditional lines.

The relevance of these issues is most certainly not restricted to The Netherlands. Recently a very inspiring paper written by John Ziman, as chairman of a Science Policy Support Group in the United Kingdom, was published. In that paper Ziman voices ideas comparable to those just mentioned, but regarding the research system in the United Kingdom.

It was exciting to have the opportunity to exchange ideas about such developments with a country like India as the first in line and compare notes as it were. The issue of cooperation between scientists from different fields where large-scale and increasingly complex problems of both a scientific and a societal nature have to be solved, in our view is an important one for science policy for the next decade.

In many areas one sees that problems can no longer be solved within the boundaries of a single discipline. I am sure you will recognize this problem. One only needs to think of the solutions which are being sought and which will be found in your brave project concerning the river Ganges. It is clear that besides technical disciplines the biological and social sciences are also of great importance in the approach to such a challenging problem.

The complexity of problems facing our societies and scientific research at large is also being increased by the fact that decisionmaking processes in our societies require an increasing amount of information. This has important consequences for the system of higher education which in addition to giving a sound training in one discipline must also further a receptiveness to results and methods of other disciplines.

The second issue mentioned concerns the movement in our society towards a new balance between the tasks of public authorities and the private-research sector. Changes in this balance that are too swift and too far reaching could lead to an irredeemable loss of expertise built up over the years and to other adverse effects.

The third issue for a science policy facing the future concerns new forms of what we call 'internationalization'. The European research landscape is changing and will change even more after the expected unification of Europe in the nineties.

Questions raised within this context are: which forms of organization are most suitable for the various parts of European research? How can a balance be achieved between centralized and national research facilities? How can strategy, financing, planning and execution of research programmes be determined in an international context? How can bureaucracy be avoided and the versatility of the research system be furthered?

Those three issues will have far-reaching consequences for the functioning of a national research system. Let me give an example. Top-management in a Dutch research organization such as TNO needs new tools to react flexibly to the changes that occur in its environment. In the past ten years such tools were introduced, for example financial schemes, a new personnel policy, and a four-year strategic plan that is discussed in Parliament. At the end of the transformation process a new law was presented to and accepted by Parliament that regulates the relationship between TNO as an independent organization and government.

So far I have spoken mainly about the content of our workshop. Now I would like to say something about its process.

It may have struck you that sometimes opinions in our delegation seemed to oppose each other. Well, Dutch people are characterized by their multitude of opinions. We even have an expression 'as many opinions as there are people'. And luckily if there is one characteristic I trust our hosts to possess, it is the talent of coping with 'ambiguity' — an 'eastern' more than a 'western' quality. So I am confident that the rich variety of opinions which we presented has not confused you too much.

Preparing a workshop on science policy is, if not a daily routine, yet a regular phenomenon on our agenda. Preparing a workshop in India, however, requires a different frame of mind. As a Dutch person one knows one will feel at home at once in India, surrounded by the warm hospitality of one's hosts. But one also has to prepare oneself for the confrontation with the incredibly large scale in quantity of people, possibilities and problems which characterize your country. Therefore one has to realize that preparation time will always be too short to even get a slight idea of the real issues that India has to deal with.

Before ending my speech, let me express our warm feelings of sympathy we all have for you. Dr Lavakare, in your person I want to thank all members of your delegation for your hospitality.

Index